Bill Barnes
1/25/93

# Converting Nine to Five

# Converting Nine to Five

## *A Spirituality of Daily Work*

John C. Haughey

Crossroad · New York

1989

The Crossroad Publishing Company
370 Lexington Avenue, New York, N.Y. 10017

Copyright © 1989 by John C. Haughey, S.J.

Printed in the United States of America

Library of Congress Cataloging-in-Publication Data

Haughey, John C.
    Converting nine to five : a spirituality of daily work / John C.
Haughey.
    p.    cm.
    Bibliography: p.
    Includes index.
    ISBN 0-8245-0945-5
    1. Work—Religious aspects—Christianity.    2. Spiritual life-
-Catholic authors.    I. Title.    II. Title: Converting 9 to 5.
BT738.5.H38    1989
248.8'8—dc20                                                89-34435
                                                           CIP

# Contents

# Introduction

This book began the day my life took an unexpected but felicitous turn. I had just written *The Holy Use of Money* and because of reactions to it found myself becoming more and more intersted in the connections between business and faith. But I was not quite sure what to do with this interest nor how to pursue it. Meanwhile, Jim Devereux, my good Jesuit provincial, and John Donoghue, the bishop of Charlotte, unbeknownst to me were conspiring to have me go to Charlotte, North Carolina. They had in mind the double task of pastoring (something I had not done in my twenty-five years of ministry) and theological reflection with business people (the very thing I found myself wanting to do).

Since my first day in Charlotte, in February 1986, I have had every opportunity imaginable to reflect with "workers" on their work. Members of Charlotte's Executive Forum and Business Guild have not known that in convening them I have also deviously functioned as a mole. I have also engaged people in reflection on the subject of work at a number of seminars throughout the country: for example, in Chicago at the Center for Ethics and Corporate Policy, in Kansas City at the Heartlands Conference, in New York at the Wall Street Round Table on Ethics, in Wernersville, Pennsylvania, at the Jesuit Spiritual Center, at Georgetown University's Seminar on Theology, at Notre Dame University, at Kirkridge, a retreat center in Bangor, Pennsylvania. The book is without statistics or surveys. It is the fruit of reflection with many.

Not a word of this book would have been written had it not been for my two Jesuit brothers with whom it is so good to live, Eugene McCreesh and Vince Alagia. Nor would one word have been typed without the meticulous skills and indefatigable zeal of Mary Ann

Twine. St. Peter's parishioners, too, have been very patient with my holing up at times, for which I am most grateful. Those who read the manuscript and offered valuable suggestions were Conrad Hoover, SO, Susan Tamborini-Martin, and Ira Hutchison. Finally, a word of gratitude to Bob Heller, who midwifed three very difficult births for me at Doubleday and has now patiently delivered this overdue near breach at the Crossroad/Continuum obstetrical unit.

# 1
# Meaning and Work

This chapter will focus on work's overall meaning. The issue can be introduced by a series of questions. Is our work meaningful? If it is not, should we change jobs to find meaningful work? Does work's meaningfulness come from the work itself or from the worker's interpretation of it? What meaning does my work have objectively? Subjectively? How important is it to us to find meaning in our work? How important should it be? What does our faith contribute to work's meaning and what can it contribute? How can we know whether our work is meaningful to God? Is there any way of understanding these questions about work's meaning?

## Five New and Four Old Sources of Meaning

Studs Terkel's fascinating interviewees work because they have to, or they want to, or a combination of the two.[1] But these possibilities only introduce the subject, they do not exhaust the meaning people attach to their work. Everyone wants meaningful work, but what makes work meaningful? Is meaning in the eye of the beholder or in the task beheld?

In his series on business psychology, Michael Maccoby's recent study *Why Work: Leading the New Generation* furnishes some interesting data for answering some of these questions.[2] He and his team surveyed more than thirty-five hundred employees at eight different companies and public-service agencies, and followed up with three hundred in-depth interviews, from 1981 to 1986. The respondents ranged from blue-collar worker to CEO.

The study focused on job motivations and it discovered eight "value drives" among the workers. These drives were for survival, relatedness, pleasure, information, mastery, meaning, play, and dignity.[3]

Maccoby and his team constructed a typology of five different types of work motivations. Each type represented a distinct way of making or finding one's work meaningful. These types are the expert, the helper, the defender, the innovator, and the self-developer.

Experts are happiest when they are sought out for their knowledge, advice, know-how, or professional skills. They are often anxious to become known and sought out not only for their particular specialization but also to become as autonomous as possible or uniquely able to handle a particular need of the company. More than half of Maccoby's interviewees admitted that becoming or remaining an expert was the most meaningful part of their work. They wanted their rewards "to represent the fair market value of their performance."[4] Unconsciously, however, they seek the reward of "parental approval."[5] Their inner reward derives from the satisfaction of having mastered a challenge or demonstrated a competence. The two most operative value drives in experts are for information and mastery.

Helper types also make work meaningful. Helpers care about people and try to humanize the bureaucratic, impersonal atmosphere of most work sites. They try to tend the wounded, smooth conflicts, and build up the bonds in work relationships. They are a significant minority in the service sector, according to this study.[6] Often reared in mother-oriented families, they tend to have as an ideal "acceptance based on common humanity within the extended family rather than on performance."[7] Formative influences in helper workers often include a strong religious background and a childhood either of scarcity or of notable abundance. There is often conflict with expert types if the helpers see them acting in an uncaring manner. Relatedness is the primary value drive of helpers.

The defender is another type of worker. Not many interviewees developed this kind of working style as a source of meaning.[8] Defenders act either as advocates for customers, clients, or subordinates, or to defend their employer against cheats or other enemies. So the defender may be either a whistle-blower crying foul or a strong promoter of the firm. The childhood of defenders is usually

deeply affected by a struggle for justice, either because they themselves were picked on unfairly or this value was strongly reinforced
by family.[9] Job satisfaction depends on getting results in the fight for
justice or in thwarting the enemy of the firm. The value drive most
operative here is the drive for dignity. Survival is a close second.

Innovators are a fourth type. They are "organizers, instigators,
and strategists."[10] Wherever and whenever they are given a chance
to be inventive or entrepreneurial they find their jobs meaningful.
When they are not, they find their job meaningless. They bring a
spirit of play to their work. Play is one of their value drives. They are
not unlike gamblers but they are usually more sophisticated and
skilled. Innovators frequently come from families that encouraged
them to be exploratory and challenged them to become indepen-
dent. As a group they were found to have the weakness of becoming
too enamored of their way of seeing and playing the game.[11]

The final type is the self-developer. Usually brought up in an
environment of considerable flux, self-developers learn early to trust
in themselves and their own abilities, which they constantly seek to
update. They thrive in organizations that stress shared responsibility
and reciprocity rather than bureaucratic or hierarchic modes of
management. They are always testing themselves and seeking to
break yesterday's boundaries.[12] Their meaning is found in developing themselves. A firm that knows how to profit from their self-
development is fortunate. A firm that thwarts their self-development
will either lose them or turn them into underinvested employees
who merely go through the motions. The self-developer seldom
makes the firm his or her whole life. They are often faithful to other
modes of self-development, such as physical exercise, diet, or hob-
bies. There is always the possibility that a self-developer is not far
from narcissism. Three value drives are usually operating in such a
type: dignity, mastery, and information.

Because of the rapidly changing contours of today's workplace,
self-developers are becoming more numerous. The traditional, industrial, hierarchically structured workplace was not a context
within which the self-developer flourished. Today's more egalitarian
structures are making it possible for this type of worker to emerge
and, frequently, succeed at what he or she deems meaningful.

I have two quibbles with Maccoby's study. One of these is that he lumps together the category of meaning with other value drives. Meaning differs from the others considerably and should not be put on a par with them. In fact, the perception of meaning lies behind each of the "value drives": information is meaningful to me because . . .; mastery is meaningful to me because . . ., and so forth. Furthermore, the term *value drives* is not helpful; these phenomena would be better named by the seldom used but highly important moral category of *affections*. Affections are the headwaters from which flows all our behavior, both good and bad. Affections are incited by objects and situations, in this case, those at work. Affections are more human and determinate than "drives." Drives connote instinct rather than feeling. Affections are also less abstract and objective than values.

Be that as it may, Maccoby's work represents a leap forward from previous efforts at understanding job motivations. The business schools and managerial courses of yesteryear had become too settled in their view of what motivated workers. As the author points out, four "partial man" theories were used for many years to explain job motivations. These theories held that money, status, power, or psychological gratification fueled workers' energies and gave work meaning.

According to this theory job motivation (and hence meaning) for "economic man" was presumed to be salary, or money in general. Since the bottom line was the focus of the corporation, the assumption was that money was the workers' bottom line. While workers do work for money, seeing money as the *sole* source of their motivation contradicts clinical evidence, according to Maccoby.[13] A partial truth becomes a falsehood when it is mistaken for the whole truth.

This problem of a partial truth posing as the whole of job meaningfulness also stalks the "sociological man" theory, wherein a person's status in the company's hierarchy or a person's success as measured by promotions was assumed to be the source of meaningfulness on the job. As long as the industrial bureaucratic structure was the norm and mass production or standardized tasks were the manner in which a given workplace operated, this view of motivation had more credibility. But new forms of business structure are coming into being because of new management theory—along with such new factors such as global competition, deregulation, telecommunications technology, and the information explosion. A new kind of work site is developing, one in which the workers get their satisfaction from the use of specialized knowledge that is usually acquired through mastery of a form of technology. Workers who are able to benefit customers and clients irrespective of their own status in a hierarchy, derive satisfaction and a sense of meaningfulness from their work.

The third notion of motivation that is also proving to be outmoded is the theory of "political man," in which power makes the job meaningful. Undoubtedly, no one can be content with powerlessness. But unlike the Machiavellian workers depicted by this theory, ordinary employees are not as interested in having power as in having a say in the conditions of the workplace that affect them and their colleagues. Although this sense of meaning is not contingent on workers' being in charge, they do need to be given some degree of ownership of the situation through which they can influence work processes and policies.

Finally, the "psychological man" theory claims people are motivated by their emotional needs. Maccoby shows that Abraham Maslow's theory of needs, for example, still influences management theory and training. Maslow holds that the lowest level of our needs is physiological, for food, drink, and sex. The next level is the need for safety. Once their physiological needs and the need for safety are satisfied, people need love and affection. The next level of need is for status, achievment, and autonomy. Finally, the last need is for creativity and self-actualization. We should be wary of Maslow's overly tidy typology and its hierarchy of needs. Such theories ignore the forces of human character, the values people embrace, their cultivated affections, and their willingness to delay or forgo meeting their needs. People will undergo great sacrifices in order to realize cherished values. As Maccoby comments, "what we choose to do depends more on our ethics than on satisfying needs."[14] We do not automatically act on the basis of needs as though we were specimens of a genetically or biologically determined infrahuman species.

## Meaningful Work and Good Work

Regarding human needs in relationship to work, E. F. Schumacher's reading is better than Maslow's. His little volume on

*Good Work* sees the worker's needs as spiritual, social, and personal.[15] Through good work we overcome our "inborn egocentricity," and bring our latent talents to realization while serving others. Through good work we learn to act on the basis of our better moral impulses and values. Through good work we learn to be creatively engaged and responsible.

Schumacher sees meaningless work as an abomination. Meaningless work is work that keeps peoples' spiritual, personal, and social needs from being met. Meaningless work is stultifying, continually boring, nerve wracking, or capable of rendering the worker a mere servant of technology. Schumacher is profoundly unimpressed by many of the benefits of the modern work situation that show concern merely for the body of the person but not the soul, which is often made ill by it. For example, the body is cared for by health and accident insurance and disability compensation. But the soul must be cared for by such things as tuition vouchers, flex time, the many forms of work-site humanization, career counseling, retirement counseling, wellness programs, and so forth. Valuable products produced by workers who are devalued while producing them are the products of disorder.

The soul of the worker is invariably made ill when work requires only the body of the worker. Work that is souless is ruinous of the soul. In *Wealth of Nations* Adam Smith describes such a situation in a pin-making factory where production was divided into eighteen different specialized tasks: "One man draws out the wire, another straights it, a third cuts it, a fourth points it," and so on.[16] What made this work meaningless (and what makes any work meaningless) is the virtual absence of selfhood required for its performance. The workers are paid for a blind pursuit of ends determined by others through the means determined by still others. No intelligence, autonomy, or initiative is asked, allowed, or expected of the workers.

Today the workplace is seldom as devoid of personal input as in Smith's day. We have made considerable progress since the industrial revolution. Most jobs have some degree of autonomy. Everyone needs to put something of their own personal stamp on their work. This implies that some degree of discretion, choice, or input is expected and called for on the job. But one's own stamp on one's work does not solve the problem of meaninglessness. One could have considerable autonomy in one's work and still find it lacking in meaning.

Schumacher brings some sense to the issue by calling for an educational process that would enable workers to discern bad work by its negative impact on them.[17] Such a process would teach a person to ask and answer four questions: What is man? Where does he come from? What purpose does his life have? What is the best means available to achieve that purpose?"[18] By dealing with these questions people would come to understand that their work must provide a means to achieve the perceived purpose of their lives in order to qualify as good work.

Schumacher is simply echoing the sentiments of many down through the ages. Thomas Aquinas, for example, observed that there would be no joy in life if there were no joy in one's work.[19] Thomas Carlyle put it this way: "He who has found his work—let him look for no other blessedness."[20] And Eric Gill lamented, "The notion of work has been separated from the notion of art. The notion of useful has been separated from the notion of the beautiful."[21]

Good work for Schumacher is work wherein some meaning is seen by and assigned to it by the worker. Objects are the stuff from which subjects make meaning. To come into ownership of our own humanity, we must make the meanings our lives have. To have objects give their meaning to us forfeits a primary function of our humanity. It is the disorder of the animals naming us rather than us the animals. Meaning cannot come from the work to the worker; it must come from the worker to the work. Meaning cannot be made by infrahuman creatures. They do not have what it takes to make meaning. Meaning making is an affective, cognitive, and evaluative process that only humans can carry out with the everyday things that come within the range of their experience.

It is not quite so simple, therefore, to say that people work either because they have to or they want to. Motivations are so much richer and complex than these two reasons, as we have already seen. If we say that one's work is either meaningless or meaningful, we erroneously locate meaning outside the person. Rather, meaning resides in workers' interpretation of their work. The exact same work can be interpreted by one person as meaningful and the other as meaningless. Granted, there is some objective basis for either judgment, something about the reality of the job itself that evokes the interpretation, but that is secondary to the dynamics within the interpreter.

The interpreter, of course, can try to wait for the work to supply meaning. This is not advisable; it will very likely be a long wait. Such an attitude allows the interpreter to assume the role of an observer, of a consumer who has to be pleased with a product, or of a victim who can indulge in self-pity. Or the interpreter can have a well-developed sense of self and autonomy, and enough self-knowledge about what he or she finds meaningful, either in a job or independently of it. This sense of self and self-knowledge are two of the keys to unlocking the treasures of job meaningfulness.

The fact that meaning requires some degree of autonomy already hints at something very important. The worker brings his or her whole self to the workplace. We can presume that every employee requires some sense of being a unique, autonomous, "me." A job has to fit this prior, already posited, and at least semideveloped sense of personhood. All of which is to say that there is already a pattern of meanings in the person who goes to work, even though it is probably largely unarticulated. No one's life is devoid of meaning: to take any action in this world, something or some things have to be seen as meaningful, others as meaningless. One's judgments might be wholly self-regarding and, therefore, meaningful only in relation to oneself. Or they can be more objective (meaningful in themselves) or social (meaningful to one's group).

One's job, if it is to have any significance in one's life, has somehow to fit into this larger sense of the meaning of one's own life. We give our work very little meaning with such judgments as, "I work just to put food on the table" or "work is a necessary evil" or "I tolerate my job because it is expected that I work." Alternately, we give our work very great meaning when we say, "I love my work" or "I am most me at my job"—in this case, work satisfies some strong affections.

Work can be meaningful intrinsically or merely extrinsically. If the former, doing the job is in itself satisfying. If the latter it is used to supply the means necessary to do the things one finds meaningful, like raising a family, getting an education, funding an interest, financing a hobby, or paying off a debt. If it is intrinsically meaningful, there can be unforeseen costs. For example, one can find work so meaningful that other things lose their appeal. Many people's marriages suffer from their overinvestment in work. In fact, people can get so immersed in their work that it begins to function like an idol. Persons who live as though they are what they do have already begun to lose their souls to the objects with which they work. No less spiritually destructive is the opposite condition: people who spend forty or more hours of the week doing something they don't like, don't respect themselves for doing, and don't see as beneficial to others, must suffer under work's negative impact on their spirits. Indeed, a cynicism and dullness of spirit that pervades the rest of life almost certainly result from this job situation.

### Meaning Making

To be human is to be a meaning maker. We do not make meaning out of thin air, of course, but with the resources we have going for us. Still, it is we who make meaning—it cannot be made for us. The grist we use for the meanings our mill makes comes from several sources: believed reports, evoked affections, and active faith.

The meanings we make are positive responses to or personal interpretations of the reports we receive from others. Sometimes the reports are intentionally communicated as meaningful, such as the reports given by parents or teachers, where persuasion, discipline, authority, and training explain much of their effectiveness. A lack of training, education, discipline, or authority might explain some of our affections for meaningless things—for objects that are of little or no worth. For the most part, therefore, meaning is mediated. Parents are mediators, but so are the media, the school, the religious institution, the peer group, the culture in all of its parts. The reports brought by mediators and the responses we give to these are the main sources of our meanings.

We never cease making meaning because we never cease receiving meanings made by others. Nor do we come to the point that we have it made once and for all. The reports never cease. They are like innumerable streams that feed into our ocean. Before the streams enter our ocean of meaning they must pass through several filters to be accepted as meaningful. The first filter, of course, is our mind. Another is our affections and a third is our faith. These latter two need some clarification.

A major source of our interpretations of meaningfulness and meaninglessness are our affections and disaffections. Affections are for objective realities, such as our spouse, family, friends, church, God, baseball, a television show, and so on. Or they can be for prized intangibles, such as recognition, achievement, power, security, or knowledge. Maccoby's value drives are affections. A person undertakes a job not with an affective tabula rasa but with a complex series of developed and developing affections. The employee will have a need to have some of these reinforced by the job. Job satisfaction has as much to do with self-knowledge (and, to be even more precise, affection-awareness) as it has to do with things we ordinarily associate with job-satisfaction like power, money, or promotions.

Affections are dispositions of the heart. They predispose us to do the things we do, make the choices we make, shape the judgments we devise, pursue the interests we are attracted to, invest the energy we invest. They are learned but are not rationally determined. They are the brute data of moral choices. To return to our metaphor of streams feeding into the ocean of meaning, affections would be positive predispositions toward certain streams. We actually seek them out. Conversely, disaffections are negative predispositions toward other streams that I have prejudged as meaningless to me.

Affections are more consistent than feelings. Feelings are more volatile and fleeting than affections. Affections are incited by objects or circumstances. If a job has neither objects nor circumstances, actual or potential, that incite a person's affections, it will be meaningless to him or her.

Affections have a close kinship to values but they also differ from them. Every affection values something "out there." Affections, however, are less objective than values. Although values are hard to define, suffice it to say here that a value is a principal, standard, object, or quality that is deemed of worth or desirable. The value of things can persist independently of the valuing subject. But nothing of affections persists independently of the subject who has them. In this sense, affections originate in the subject while values result from the subject's response to objects. I can highly value objects for which I have slight or no affection, for example, prayer, fine art, classical music, or the virtue of compassion. And I can have an affection for an object I do not value, like a team I follow but despise or a television show I blame myself for wasting time on. We esteem things of value but we act on our affections.

Affections, however, are not wholly subjective, as can be attested by our educational systems, fine-arts associations, and religious institutions. All of these industries, if we may call them that, know that affections can be cultivated for objects that are of value. The cultivation of affections has as much to do with the process of education as the cultivation of the mind with ideas. Though this aspect of education is seldom adverted to, it is the core of moral formation. Our moral character is only as good as our loves and loathings.

Most employers ignore their employees' affections. But if the employees' affections are incited for something job-related, enormous energy for the company results. If there is no affectivity elicited, the employer or manager should not be surprised if employees are simply putting in their time, going through the motions, punching the clock. "No affection for" translates into "it has no meaning for me" or "it is a meaningless job." Even when a job is valued objectively, such as teaching, nursing, or other jobs in the service professions might be, there is no guarantee that something workers see as objectively valuable will also be an object of their affections.

## Transcendent Meanings of Work

Almost all the meanings we assign to our work are immanently arrived at and immanently construed. *Immanent* (in contrast to *transcendent*) means here that the assigned meaning is secular, its horizon is in the world of the here and now, and its explanation derives from the immediate matrix of the worker's reality. All of Maccoby's types, for example, assigned immanent meanings to their work satisfactions and motivations.

The transcendent meaning of one's work can arise in two different ways. One way for work to have transcendent meaning develops when the worker takes on an agenda that transcends his or her personal benefits and satisfactions in doing the work. When workers go beyond the tasks enumerated in their job descriptions or assume responsibilities related to but exceeding their assigned work, they have begun to find a transcendent meaning in their work. The other way for work to have transcendent meaning develops when one can connect it with his or her religious faith.

The first form of transcendence touches on all the hopes and dreams people have about what their workplace might or ought to become. These might be about worker ownership or worker participation, employee rights or employee benefits, economic justice or profit sharing, consumer protection or job safety, pay raises or credit-union investments, a merger or a divestiture, and so forth. The point here is that the worker is working at something that transcends his or her personal satisfactions and benefits: since the hoped-for benefits are for many, the worker is self-transcending by taking on this additional responsibility.

What is purused in transcendence need not be something on a grand scale. It can be a specific cause or goal. Causes or goals are effective sources of meaning if the means for promoting or achieving them are known and available to those who would pursue them. But the agenda may be larger than something that can be achieved by concerted action focused on a specific goal in a local situation. Worker democracy or overcoming sexism in the workplace are two of these larger agendas whose realization is considerably more complex than that of specific goals. Such a larger agenda would require a conversion of minds, hearts, and attitudes in most cases to bring the dream to realization. Overcoming most forms of discrimination, especially those that are embedded in our society, requires dreamers with unfailing commitment to the dreams.

Working to realize a dream larger than oneself and one's loved ones can give one's work, not to mention one's life, new meaning. It can release enormous moral energy to launch each new campaign of action and suffer each new set of resistances. Dreams of justice are ordinarily met with the enormous resistance of those who benefit from the present arrangement of things and who have every reason to dig in their heels when their interests are threatened by dreams of redistribution, vindication, or participation engendered in the hearts of workers.

Here I wish neither to evaluate particular causes or larger dreams, nor to judge their validity. All I wish is to establish the point that when workers adopt goals that involve either structural changes in the manner in which work is performed and compensated or systemic changes in the work site, such goals can become fonts of new meaning for workers because they enable them to transcend themselves and pursue courses of action beyond their personal aspirations, ambitions, interests, or goals.

Dreams, which invariably involve struggle against the present arrangement, differ from goals that can be achieved by a rearrangement of the present parts. Dreams are less rational than goals. That is why they have to be dreamt, in order to have content. Dreams can evoke the whole person in a way that goals do not always succeed at doing. One need only think of the degree of moral energy that was released by the Solidarity movement in Poland during the 1970s to realize how the meaning-making power of dreams like this can awaken the heart. The level of felt meaning among those who work with a dream to be realized—a dream that is larger than themselves, to which they are passionately attracted, and in view of which they take actions—cannot be compared with the different level of felt meaning among those who work without a dream, who work for the smaller agendas that come from themselves, their needs, the needs of their families.

Think of the energies released by present dreams in our world, e.g., the energy to act against the violations of personal dignity in South Africa and Israel, Latin America's repressive regimes, or the Soviet Union's human rights violations, to mention only a few. Dreams are usually born in circumstances in which injustice is rife. Solidarity is achieved with relative ease when many people share a perception of injustice and are prepared to work for its eradication and for a new day when wrongs are righted. The cost of doing nothing is seen to be greater than the cost of doing whatever it takes to realize the new day and the justice that accompanies it. Whole movements arise from the leadership of a few who first dare to dream. Across the globe, tens of thousands of political prisoners who have taken action at great cost to themselves are testimony to the power of a dream of justice. Their examples are more stark than those we find in American work situations, since our workplace injustices are usually less blatant and the actions taken to realize justice for workers are usually politically less harsh.

Lest all this sound one-sided or like an antibusiness, antimanagement tirade, we should note that managers and owners are not without their larger-than-life dreams. These can be for creating more jobs, for a greater sharing of the profits for their employees, for a more affordable service to their customers, or for products that will save their clients money or grief. They can be for less regulation or more regulation, a cleaner environment, more tariffs or less protectionism, and so forth. The manager or owner who dreams of greater benefits for others—whether those others be the public, the consumers, employees, or colleagues—is living for a larger purpose than his or her own benefit.

Whether we are talking about owners, managers, or the rank-and-file work force, considerable moral energy and, therefore, meaning are lost when dreams are shattered. When "realism" takes over and, for whatever reasons, a dream cannot be realized, the zeal and zest that were generated by the dream evaporate and meanings shrink. There is also a danger that all meaning will vanish. An enormous moral tragedy ensues when a person, group, or community loses its ability to sustain a dream.

## Making Religious Meaning

Religion, with its visions of transcendence, is the final source of meaning we will consider. Historically, religious faith has been the major source of the meanings people put on their lives and the things they do. If the job one does is unconnected with the faith one adheres to, the job will be unconnected with a major source of its potential meaning. The job's meaning, therefore, will be merely immanent, confined to a smaller sphere of reality than one believes exists. Such confinement is unnecessary and wrongheaded. It serves neither the employer nor the employee nor those served by the work done.

People of religious faith usually try to make sense of what they do by finding more-than-immanent meaning in it. They do not always

succeed. They can hardly be satisfied by merely immanent meanings if they are trying to live their faith. Faith is meant to open the
things that occupy us in this world to a transcendent horizon. The
desired consequence of this deeper, longer, taller, wider perspective
is that everyday things will fit into it. Everyday things, of course,
will also retain their immanent meanings. The transcendent does
not ordinarily cancel the immanent meanings we find in things.
Faith gives us a transcendent horizon with which we can construe
the meanings of things differently than do those who know only
immanent meanings.

A combination of immanent and transcendent meanings augurs
well for a healthy faith. A person's faith would be grotesque if the
only meanings he or she attached to things were of a transcendental
character. This would be the error of "integralism," which means the
effort to explain or master an understanding of reality exclusively
in the light of faith. In matters germane to our study, integralism
would mean that one could see in daily work no meaning for oneself
or for the enterprise for which one worked unless it somehow or
other cashed out in terms of eternity. People with this mentality
would hardly make good employees. They could hardly be trusted
with the things of time, being so preoccupied with the heavenly
merits or rewards they were gaining. No less deficient (and more
frequently the case) is a faith that sees no connection between
earthly, everyday things and the transcendent horizon of faith. This
schizophrenic condition develops when one's faith has been badly
weakened by cultural secularism or by an educational background
that was wholly secular. Ideally, the person of faith finds the world
filled with meaningful things, and does any number of things that
are meaningful to him or her, both immanently and transcendently.

Some examples will help us see how the resources available to
people of religious faith can be used to uncover the transcendent
meaning in that which may have an immanent meaning already in
place. We will now examine in this regard some of the scriptural
themes that can open up a transcendent horizon and give new
meaning to one's everyday work.

## The Call

One may see what one does, including work, as a response to
God's call. More specifically, the "Come, follow me!" of Christ

extends to the person and includes his or her work. Action taken on
the basis of a call heard is a source of considerable meaning. When
the many bends and turns in one's daily work are seen as part of
following Christ, then one's work can be constantly refreshed by a
transcendent meaning.

### One Who Serves

The theme of service can take several forms. One of these is the
imitation of Christ himself, who characterized himself in these
terms: "The Son of Man did not come to be served but to serve"
(Matt. 20:28). Another form is an active belief in the inviolable
dignity of the human person who is made in God's image and
likeness. The appropriate response to such an exalted other,
whether colleague or client or boss or customer, would be a deep
reverence and an attitude of service. A third form is to see that other
as Christ himself and serve him by meeting his needs for food,
drink, clothing, and so forth (the classical text for this begins with
Matt. 25:31).

### Eucharist

There are many aspects of the rich theology of the Eucharist that
are appropriate to one's daily work. The simplest of these is that of
offering oneself as bread to be broken that others may eat: "Unless
the grain of wheat . . ." (John 12:24). Another is the theme of
participation in the mediatorship of Christ. By baptism the Christian has been made a participant in the priesthood of Christ, and
this power is exercised by offering to God through Christ all we do,
including what is done by the larger whole of which one is a part.
The transformation of the world by its reconciliation with Christ
through the self-offering of the members of his body can be a major
source of transcendent meaning in one's job. We will see some of
this in Teilhard de Chardin's insights in chapter six.

### Co-Creators

The worker can see the materials worked with in terms of their
source, the Creator, and can hear the commission to transform them

in all the ways that bring them to their full potential. The worker can see the tasks to be done as a matter of picking up where God leaves off. The dreamer sees God's bounty as plentiful but unevenly distributed and, therefore, as needing a more equitable distribution. The scientist attempts to pierce the secrets of the universe to the inner workings with which God has scripted them. The engineer, doctor, entrepreneur, miner, parent, craftsmen, and so on, are able to see how they are co-creators with God in the tasks they have to do in this world.

### Stewardship

Stewardship is a variation on the co-creator theme. The steward of God's creation knows full well that "the earth is the Lord's and its fullness" (Ps. 24:1). It is clear to stewards that what they have, they have in trust. Their work, then, is a service of God. By taking it as their responsibility to develop the earth's resources, they serve God and God's purposes. The parable of the tenant farmers is a rich source for reflecting on how not to be a steward: the tenants forgot whose vineyard they were working in and came to a sorry end (Matt. 21:33–43).

### Curse

The curse in Genesis is a considerable resource for perceiving the transcendent meanings of daily work: "By the sweat of your brow you shall get to eat bread" (Gen. 3:19). Any drudgery or monotony or ordeal experienced at work can be traced to the original cleavage we call the Fall. Hassles take on a meaning beyond the here and now. Such a perspective may not alleviate the hassle but it can give it a meaning beyond itself.

### Covenant

Covenant is one of the richest themes in all of Scripture for giving perspective and new meaning to daily work. It assumes the other themes and makes them more intimate. God has reached out and made a pact with a people. Being a member of that people with

whom God is covenanted invites a drastic rethinking of the meaning
of salaried employment. Specifically, this means I work for God and
commit myself to him; God also is committed to me and works on
my behalf. The totality of the covenant means that one has already
been "spoken for" and is no longer available to become the slave of
another master. (For God's covenant with Noah, see Gen. 9; with
Abraham, Gen. 17; with the Israelite slaves in Egypt, Exod. 6;
with Moses and Israel on Sinai, Exod. 34; and for the fullest treatment of covenant, the passage that begins at Deut. 4:44.)

### New Heavens/New Earth

The theme of new heavens and new earth, in its deeper significance, does not mean that all things in time (including our work)
must be judged in light of their eternal significance for our souls.
The spiritual teachings of old used the Latin phrase *sub specie
aeternitatis* ("in light of eternity"). This led one to ask, What does
this or that action taken in time mean in the light of eternity? This
implies a dated world-despising view of time, history, and our efforts
in the world. The deeper meaning of eschatology for Christians is
that they already possess the life which is eternal. They do not await
it. They *do* await its fullness, or resplendent release, throughout
reality made new gradually over time by, through, and in Christ (2
Pet. 3:13).

### Justice

Justice is certainly one of the richest themes in scripture for
giving meaning to work. With this theme the dignity of persons is
front and center in God's plan, and hence in ours, if we allow
ourselves to take on God's agenda. The future definitive reign of God
is depicted repeatedly in Scripture as having justice as its primary
ingredient and content. Augurs of this justice are possible and
necessary in time if those of no belief or weak belief are to come to
believe that our life and work have meaning. The definitive reign of
God needs midwives to help usher its provisional instances into
time and, specifically, into the workplace. Workplace justice is not
beyond the reach of human beings: Jesus' own ministry is one long
record of his effort to effect the transformation of a social context

from one in which people's dignity is denied to one in which it is affirmed.

In brief, our contention is that the maker of meaning is the person and the meanings we make are considerably richer when we use the categories of faith we have inherited from our religious tradition. If we do not employ them, our work is needlessly impoverished. If our work's meanings are merely immanent, work weakens our spiritual condition by reinforcing a split consciousness. If the meaning of our work is thin, vague, or virtually nonexistent, the money we earn will be the sole and final meaning of our work, and we will be left with a void of meaning. This is a dangerous spiritual condition to be in.

If salary is the sole, or even primary, measure of work's meaning, we are in a pathetic condition. The worker who sees no more meaning in work than money will soon be alienated since his or her work has been virtually emptied of value.

# 2

# The Creator God
# and Working People

Even though a spirituality of work must be experience based and composed by working people themselves, input is needed of a religious or theological character. This input can come from something as simple as a verse of Scripture or advice from a friend. Or it can come from something more fulsome like the elaboration of a pertinent theme from Scripture or tradition. In the remaining chapters we will attempt to meet the reader's need for a fuller theological treatment first by examining the creation myth and its implication for our work.

### Alienation

Perhaps the major tension in the majority of workplaces is that between alienation and dominion. Alienation is an experience. Dominion is a call, as I hope to show. The tension between these two can be considerable because somehow we seem to know that we were meant to take dominion over things. But the experience of most people, especially in our work situations, is the opposite of this, namely, things take dominion over us.

This chapter will first inquire into alienation. It will then offer a brief meditation on the Genesis account of creation. And finally it will explore the significance of the commission given Adam and Eve in the garden. The Genesis text roots the meaning of human work in the intentions of God prior to the fall from grace. Without the myth of the fall it would be hard to explain why work (and everything else we try to do) is so fraught with problems. Without the myth of creation it would be hard to establish a foundation for the dignity of work.

There is virtually no literature about work that neglects to mention alienation. Karl Marx gave the term its currency in connection with work. Alienation developed, he contended, when workers were separated from their work, from what they produced, and from one another. The worker "is separated from his work [he plays no part in deciding what to do or how to do it]."[1] This severs him from the activity that makes him who he is. He is also separated "from his own products [he has no control over what he makes or what becomes of it afterward], causing a break between the individual and the material world."[2] And, finally, "he is separated from his fellow men [competition and class hostility have rendered most forms of cooperation impossible], causing a break between man and man."[3] In the majority of nineteenth-century workers Marx saw individuals who were splintered into so many misbegotten parts of a greater whole. The several levels of splintering, all experienced most acutely in the workplace, created a new anthropological phenomenon, "alienated man."

More recent studies have tended to examine alienation more in psychological terms than in Marx's structural or systemic terms. The symptoms of alienation are not wholly agreed upon by these psychological studies but there are some commonly noted symptoms that verify the presence of the condition.[4] These symptoms are, first of all, a feeling of powerlessness because "I am unable to influence my work situation." There is a feeling of normlessness. The only norm guiding the work seems to be "produce and you will be paid." Other principles seems nonexistent. There is a feeling of isolation: "I don't see that I matter to anyone, nor do I have a sense of belonging. The organization is uninterested in me and, therefore, I feel wholly uninvested in it." There is a feeling of being instrumentalized: "I don't want to be treated like an instrument. The result is that I *use* the work more than *do* the work. I have decided to have other fish to fry with the salary I receive. I feel like I'm playing a game." Deep down, it's hard to take something seriously when you are not taken seriously. You learn to play the game by the rules so that you don't lose, not because winning is worth anything.

Many of the complex causes of alienation can be found in the structures of modern life, especially in the manner in which work tends to be done. These external structures, in turn, shape the phenomenon of psychic alienation, some of whose symptoms are described above. Erich Fromm was one of the first to describe the psychological condition of alienation from oneself, which is a feeling of estrangement from one's own inmost self.[5] He saw this pathology as directly traceable to the structures of modern life. When one's social context is unstable and fragmented, the process of healthy individuation is imperiled. The result is diffuse and confused identities who are estranged from themselves even before they enter the job market.

Some of the structural causes of alienation are:

1. Bureaucracy: Needless complexity and proliferation of structures distance workers from one another and from those who shape the work. Bureaucracy's centralization and formalization of tasks and projects makes for dissatisfaction. It reduces the workers' sense that they are contributing something unique to the common project.

2. Division of labor: The specialization of functions each worker performs makes for stultification; so small a part of the person is utilized that the rest remains undeveloped; resentment of the cause of this situation is traced to the workplace.

3. Mergers and acquisitions: In recent years there has been such a massive restructuring of corporate America that even the management class, where alienation was rarer, is beginning to be impacted by all the feelings of alienation that so many nonmanagement employees experienced. Stability, predictability, loyalty, and commitment are all seriously jeopardized by massive corporate restructuring.

4. Automation and technology: Many workers sense that they can be replaced at any time by some new technological advance. This surely adds nothing to one's sense of worth at one's job. Part of this sense of being obsolete is generational: workers of the younger generation are more skilled at the use of newer technologies or are more desirable because entry-level salaries are lower.

5. Discrimination: The realization that one is undervalued or disqualified by virtue of gender, race, or age creates a bewildering sense of impotence and outrage. Less frequently, ethnic, religious,

or class factors can also be at play. Any one of these situations can cause a sense of alienation.

6. "Macro-ometry": This word is coined to describe the feeling that "it's all too much to understand or too out of hand to bring to order." It is too much, in a word. The internationalization of the economy and the rapid changes in the finance industry, as just two examples, are bewildering enough to have led many, even in the scholarly community, to a feeling that sense can no longer be made of the human project, either in its macrosystems or in the micro-systems that are impacted by the macrosystems.

The consequences of alienation beyond those already mentioned are not hard to guess. Those afflicted usually turn in on themselves in some way. These inward turns take the form of cynicism or inferiority or despair or hostility or a sense of fatalism. Marx tried to project the effects of alienation outward, into rage at the capitalist system, which he saw as their cause. Today there is not much appetite for this reaction, at least among the present generation of Americans.

The most frequent reaction to the causes of alienation seems to be logical rather than psychological. The logic is subtle and not reflec-tive. It runs something like this: "Since 'it' doesn't make sense or since I am not appreciated 'out there,' I will retreat into my own self-interested world and milk the outside world for all it's worth (which, as far as I can see, isn't very much)." Americans are famous for their individualism. In some cases, individualism isn't so much a choice as it is a reaction to having tried to make it "out there" and finding "it" too confounding to invest oneself in any depth.

The healthiest but maybe one of the less frequent responses to the causes of alienation is to commit oneself to changing the conditions that breed alienation in the workplace.


## A Theology of Work

In what follows I will develop a theological rationale for work. It will have as a secondary purpose the development of a theological antidote to alienation. (I am aware that some alienation can be handled only clinically or therapeutically. In such cases, therefore, theology cannot be helpful.)

The alienated one has lost his or her place in the world. It is helpful to return to the creation myth to reroute oneself in the world, to rediscover the place of work in the world, and to hear again the vocation God gave to all who come into this world.

The first thing this exercise calls for is a slow, image-filled reading of the first chapter of the Book of Genesis. The important thing to remember about entering into a symbolic text is that it invites freedom and imagination before analysis and thought. Thought can emerge once the symbol is entered and the imagination is stimulated by it. "The symbol gives rise to thought," Paul Ricoeur reminded a whole world of would-be analysts.[6]

The first and most imposing symbol in this chapter is of a very energetic and resourceful God. This God of Genesis is inventive, committed, busy, and productive. This God immensely enjoys the work of bringing order out of chaos and having this order filled with every imaginable kind of creature. An almost profligate kind of enjoyment is evident as God the Creator makes the sea teem with every kind of swimming thing, even "great sea monsters," while the earth brings forth all kinds of creeping things and winged things under night and day.

In the midst of all this fecundity and creativity God decides to create two creatures, one male, one female. They are made in God's own image and likeness. Man and woman have been fashioned according to the image of the creator God, the producer God, the resourceful God. Before there is any theologizing about our humanity (or any anthropology, for that matter), it is good to sit and taste this wondrous assertion that the image God had in making us was God's self. Man and woman, unlike any other creature, were and are made "in our image, after our likeness" (Gen. 1:26). But what is this image and likeness? The test doesn't leave us guessing. The God who works creates a man and woman who are to be chips off the old block. They, too, will playfully work.

Before there is a fall or sin or moral trauma, there is the very productive God calling into being special creatures who are to pick up with their productivity where God left off. This is so primary, elemental, even primitive, that it can be and usually is overlooked,

even by those who know much about Scripture. If the Creator
fashioned man and woman according to the image of the Creator in
the inspired text, then this is a very important datum. God is not
portrayed in this text as distant and contemplative, but as productive, working, and industrious.

We need to be as concrete as the text is. God is asking the man
and the woman to be like God in a particular way. They are to have
dominion over the creatures God made. "Let them have dominion
over the fish of the sea, the birds of the air, and the cattle, and over
all the wild animals and all the creatures that crawl on the ground"
(Gen. 1:26). A variation on this is they are "to cultivate the garden
and care for it" (Gen. 2:15).

If a symbol is to give rise to thought, then the thought that easily
emerges at this point in our meditation is that we are meant to take
possession of our humanity and our world by bringing them to
realization by what we make, do, work at, work on, and produce
with the means that God puts at our disposal. In other words, as we
shape and do things, they make us who we are. Conversely, inactivity and nonproductivity leave the person unmade, half-made, or
misshapen. If the cause of the inactivity is structural, like unemploy-
ment, this must be seen as an important flaw in society since it is
deeply disfiguring of the person who was made in God's own image
and likeness. If the cause of the inactivity is a personal moral flaw,
like indolence or sloth, this, too, must be named for what it is. My
own observation is that one of the major causes of workplace alienation, sloppy work, and underinvestment in work on the part of many
otherwise religious people is that they have not seen or been taught
the connection between daily work and God's intentions in making
us.

We never cease to make ourselves according to the image we have
of ourselves. As people of faith we know we are to make ourselves
according to the image God gives us of who we are. But, wonder of
wonders, that image is to be located in revelation's disclosures of
who God is. That image isn't up for grabs here. Here is a Creator
who creates, produces, works—in a word, takes dominion. Here is a
creature made in the image of this God to whom God gives dominion over what God has made. What could be clearer?

How God took dominion and in what this dominion consists are the next points of curiosity. Given the nature of the Genesis text, we know we are working with neither facts nor history but with myth and symbol. The text is suggestive and evocative, giving hints, not didactic and instructional, giving truths. The text describes what God did in the six days of creation. "In the beginning when God created the heavens and the earth, the earth was a formless wasteland, and darkness covered the abyss" (Gen. 1:1–2). God intervened again and again. "Let there be . . . and there was. . . ." Where there was formless waste and darkness God interjected form and order. Where there was abyss, God filled it with living and nonliving things each doing its own thing.

The manner in which God worked was to create and to assume dominion over these creatures. While God's human creatures can't create as God did, they can be resourceful and creative with all the things God has made. They are called to do just that by cultivating the garden with seeds they didn't make, and so forth. They are not invited to create but they are asked to assume dominion, taking up where God chose to leave off. What specifically can this mean?

Although the text isn't meant to answer a question like that, it nevertheless prompts the question. It also gives us some handle to get to the beginnings of an answer. Yahweh started with three predominion conditions: formlessness, primeval darkness, and the abyss. Dominion must mean bringing form to formlessness, fecundity to waste, and content to a void.

Putting form where there is formlessness is something we do every day. It might involve something as simple as straightening the desk or making the bed. More importantly, it means establishing or conforming to habits or schemes whereby things that need to be done regularly can be done in a recurring way more easily because of the habits, schemes, or systems imposed on them. Lonergan's distinction between a good of desire and a good of order is helpful here.[7] A good of desire is a good that satisfies a particular need. A good of order is a scheme imposed on what would otherwise have to be given order again and again. Goods of order are systems for insuring goods of desire on a recurring basis. Goods of order make it possible for us to satisfy our needs for goods of desire. Goods of order are largely taken for granted, as they should be, until they malfunction for whatever reason. Then we know how good they were and how necessary dominion is.

With this simple distinction, one could profitably look around and marvel at the dominion humans have succeeded at bringing to the human enterprise. They have established an almost infinite number of goods of order, bringing form where there was formlessness or deficiency of form. We are the rich beneficiaries of innumerable forebears who wittingly or unwittingly obeyed the command of the Lord given to the species to have dominion over the things God's hands have made.

These assertions do not appear explicitly in the biblical text, but they follow logically and spell out some of the implication of the primordial human vocation to take dominion over creation. One way to take dominion is to bring light, the light of insight or understanding, into darkness. It might be a matter of the darkness of my own ignorance and the enlightening may be just for me. Or it might be a more general darkness and the enlightening may be for many. It is even possible that everyone is in darkness and the needed light is for all. Whichever, the enlightening of any area of darkness is an action of dominion over ignorance that imitates the One in whose image and likeness we were made. After all, God didn't make the darkness but rather confined it or dispelled it with light.

The abyss is another image in these first verses of Genesis that could be used to suggest the forms of dominion that are within reach of all who have been made in the image and likeness of God. I see an abyss as an absence of an achievable competence. Abysses can be filled. Any number of technical competences can be acquired to extend the area of dominion in one's own life or in the areas in which one works or relates to others. Who hasn't suffered under incompetence almost daily, through others' incompetences or our own that keep us from contributing to the well-being of others?

All the ways of taking dominion over a few things or many things, as God gives us to do, stave off the encroaching chaos and reversion to formlessness that stalks our world and our persons. When our ancestors were first given the invitation to take dominion, they were in an idyllic enclosed orchard (as the Garden was literally described), from which they and we have been expelled. Although we

now labor in a spot "east of Eden" (Gen. 3:23), the vocation remains.
The invitation has never been retracted. The command has never
been rescinded.

God's work was not completed on the sixth day. On the eighth day,
so to speak, it came close to being undone. The effective attainment
of dominion by every human being who comes into the world is
another step toward the completion of creation. Every instance of
dominion neglected or negligently pursued, delays or retards the
completion. We inherit goods of order, the lights and the competencies of our predecessors. They invite us to stamp them with further
form and order. There is no guarantee that this will take place.
Anyone can be the author of a reversion to chaos and formlessness.
These reversions can be micro or they can be macro: a person can
become a drug addict, a bank can go belly up, a spaceship can
explode at take off, a nation can initiate war, an ocean can become
polluted, a species can become extinct.

People have always intuitively known that creation is unfinished.
It is only in this century that we have come to know that creation can
be undone by us. We can fall back into a formless wasteland and
darkness can cover the abyss because of weapons of mass destruc-
tion. But along with destructive weaponry, there is also the threat of
massive ecological damage from the pursuit of life-styles we have
come to take for granted. Think of the ozone layer, for example, and
the threat its depletion poses. By our failure to understand it, we
have not taken the dominion over it that we must now assume. Acid
rain, the greenhouse effect, the dangers of nuclear power, toxic-
waste disposal are other problems caused by twentieth-century
society's inadequate grasp of our world and the knowledge we need
to take dominion of it. Dominion is no longer an ideal for a few of the
religiously fervent. It is a necessity for life on the planet.

But we need not take in such a wide panorama to see some of the
dramatic tensions between worker's alienation and this commission
to take dominion. Alienation is winning out wherever we wait for
"meaningfulness" to come from the work itself. This is akin to having
the animals name Adam. Dominion, on the other hand, wins out
when we name the animals, that is, when we assign meaning to the
work we do. Alienation occurs when we assume that there is nothing
we can do about the encroaching chaos in the work site, that we are

powerless to bring order to chaos. When the economy and its bottom-line considerations take priority over labor, dominion's commission is being disobeyed. Dominion is achieved wherever there is a refusal to acquiesce in the feeling of powerlessness about political, economic, corporate, and occupational chaos. Action is then taken in whatever form it takes to achieve order. Alienation proliferates where there is a dearth of purpose. The abyss is filled with entry of purpose. Dominion wins when work becomes purposeful, when we take the measure of it, not it the measure of us.

## Mistaken Forms of Dominion

If dominion is misconstrued it can easily be confused with various forms of domination. Domination is, among other things, the unjust imposition of one's will on others. Domination treats subjects (persons) like objects (things). Dominion, in contrast, treats objects like objects and subjects as equals. The commission to dominion is relative not absolute. Only God has absolute dominion over creatures. But even God's absolute dominion is not exercised by domination. God created man and woman as subjects not objects. Subjects, human subjects, were made to shape objects. Even when they were cast out of Eden they were not made objects by God, although through their sins they frequently treated each other as objects.

When sin entered the world, dominion as a vocation became confused with domination as an exigency. Dominion was meant to result in mastery and order, not control and attempts at subjugation. Mistaken forms of dominion are especially evident in four different places: the environment, the economy, the relationship between the sexes, and in many work situations.

Let us look first at the mistaken form of dominion in the exploitation of nature. We have already made mention of acid rain, the greenhouse effect, and ozone-layer depletion. Some of the wounds we have inflicted on the order of nature were unintended and due to our ignorance. Others were wanton. In both cases, we are reminded by disastrous consequences that the things over which we have been given dominion have their own fragile existence and exigencies. Mishandled dominion comes from being ignorant of the nature of the things we are to handle. Awareness of our ignorance and reverence for the sacred character of all of God's creatures are two attitudinal prerequisites for a proper attitude of dominion over nature.

Ecological ethics is becoming an important part of the field of ethics. Without pausing to illustrate its growing dimensions, it would be instructive to point out that the spirituality of the first inhabitants of our country, whom we are prone to call primitive savages, made ecological ethics unnecessary. Theirs was a profound insight into the sacred character of God's creatures, in contrast to us moderns who presume to be more spiritually sophisticated. A century ago, Chief Seattle of the Squamish Indians sounded the alarm of his people about the coarseness of the white man's attitude toward nature:

> How can you buy or sell the sky, the warmth of the land? . . . Every shining pine needle, every sandy shore, every mist in the dark wood, every clearing and humming insect is holy in the memory and experience of my people. . . . The rivers are our brothers, they quench our thirst. . . . I have seen a thousand rotting buffaloes on the prairie, left by the white man who shot them from a passing train.
>
> What is man without the beasts? If all the beasts were gone, men would die from a great loneliness of spirit. For whatever happens to the beasts soon happens to man. All things are connected.[8]

Another misinterpretation of dominion has to do with the economy. The most obvious form of this is greed. When one strives for more than what is necessary to live a decent life and raise a family in a decent manner, there will be disorder. When one puts one's trust in financial security or seeks to amass enough to achieve invulnerability from human limitation, then dominion has been misconstrued again. Jesus described this misconstrual in terms of Mammon. Mammon is a creature which poses as being worthy of limitless trust. It usurps the role of the Fatherhood of God. This counterfeit object of trust wreaks havoc on the order God intends for those to whom dominion is given.[9]

But there is another disorder with respect to the economy that is much subtler. We know in the abstract that people must take priority over things. But in the concrete, when we specify workers, those who labor, as people and specify capital as things, the principle is almost universally taken to be inapplicable. But of all the places where labor should have priority over capital it would seem to be most appropriate in matters of business, commerce, and industry. Operationally, however, capital increasingly holds sway over labor. Human dignity is yielded across the board to capital. Money talks. We act like mutes before its imperious voice. Maximizing profits and the bottom line take priority over people. People's needs are being brought before the bench of capital and found guilty of public disorder. But this is a great travesty of justice and a reversal of the right order of things. People were given stewardship over the goods of the earth and the wealth that derives from the use of those goods. Wealth was not given stewardship over people.

Yet another misconstrual of dominion is in relationships between people. We have advanced sufficiently in civilization to discard the social convention of slavery. We have also begun to give a closer hearing to human rights, for the most part accepting political rights in theory but balking at the notion of socioeconomic rights.[10] When both of these sets of rights, political and economic, find their way into public policy and international law, that day will be a day of rejoicing. It will be a day when the Word of God spoken in the beginning about our being made in God's image and likeness, will have taken on the flesh of statute in human interaction. Accepting the theory and living according to it in practice will be a great leap forward in the human race's taking its God-given dominion seriously.

The most ingrained habits in contemporary society show how easy it is to misconstrue self-images, God images, and, consequently, relationships among people. These habits have been variously called patriarchy or androcentrism or sexism. No matter what term one wishes to use, the problem is very real and very much with us. The exercise of domination by one gender over another, however subtly it is done, is morally wrong. No such order was assigned in this text. "God blessed them [male and female], saying: 'Be fertile and multiply; fill the earth and subdue it. Have dominion . . .'" (Gen. 1:28). Not only was there a single commission that was to be shouldered equally by both, but they could not have carried out the commission without one another. Their sexual complementarity made them coproducers in this drama that had all the things of time and earth as their props.

Sexism is a major cause of our reading into God things that God does not say about being God. It projects into God things that in our fallen state we want God to be so that we can legitimate what we want to be. Into God has been projected the personhood of a potentate rather than of a provider, a patriarch rather than a nurturer, a dominator rather than a creator who invites us into shared dominion. One contribution of good feminist thinking is that we have come to see more clearly how civilization has misread what is being communicated about God in the Scriptures. Such feminist analysis has unearthed the long-buried feminine qualities of God.[11] It has also pointed out the masculine and feminine archetypal psychic energies that need to operate in all healthy individuals. Without their mutual operation, individual personalities and whole societies suffer from dominion run amok into sexism, sexual inequity, and sexual exploitation. The centures-old repression by males and by societies of the feminine in themselves has served to dehumanize society. It has often made domination a desirable goal. Militarism is the most ready example at hand of the consequences of this repression.

We are far beyond the industrial revolution and its harsh domination of labor. So we can't point to that history as a sign of a problem. Furthermore, we can point to many improvements in contemporary business culture, such as collective bargaining and better management theory and practice, that indicate a change from the harshness of earlier industrial nonrelations. There is still a long way to go, however, before dominion is achieved. Take, for example, the participation of workers in the decisions that shape their work. This is still inadequate.[12] The massive restructuring of corporate America, furthermore, is going on largely without the voice of labor. The weakening of labor and the trade unions has not helped workers to have a voice in the restructuring. Labor has been victimized by the domination of owners and managers, but it has also been frequently guilty of trying to dominate its own members. There has also been too much deference paid by corporate America to shareholders' interests at the expense of the stakeholders.[13] This is also a form of domination that needs to be addressed. Workers' rights are still in their infancy in this country.[14] But workers' responsibilities to employers also have a long way to go. In brief, if we use the dominion paradigm to measure industrial relations we have come only a little distance.

### Why So Many Misfires?

Reflective Christians should find a ready answer to the question of misfires in the protological myths of their tradition. The terrible moral trauma of the fall from grace of our first parents caused the dominion commission (which was never retracted) to be twisted by their progeny. We have examined two of the effects of the Fall: alienation, and the propensity to mistake domination for dominion.

Three authors have insights into this issue of dominion versus domination. In a treatise that deeply affects our view of work and our image of ourselves, the 1981 encyclical *On Human Work*, Pope John Paul II distinguished two aspects of work: subjective and objective. He insists that

> the basis for determining the value of human work is not primarily
> the kind of work being done but the fact that the one doing it is a
> person. The sources of the dignity of work are to be sought principally
> in the subjective dimension, not in the objective . . . work is for man
> not man for work.[15]

The pope's concern is warranted. The value of human work is constantly measured from the side of the objects produced, not from the side of the producers. People, consequently, are invariably evaluated for what they can do and do do, and it is not a long leap to the view that others and oneself are merely pieces of the whole complex means of production. Everyone is demeaned by such an assessment.

The human person must be seen as "subject and maker and the true purpose of the whole process of production."[16] One must not accept a view in which the objective side of work is strongly prized to the jeopardy of the subjective aspect. One must mobilize one's own inner resources to resist internalizing the demeaning attitude with which one might succumb to the consequences of this mistaken assignment of worth. Refusing to devalue others is also essential. And, finally, mobilizing one's colleagues to resist this devaluation and reject this demonic criterion is a third response. The trade union movement came into being because of those who chose not to acquiesce in the prizing of capital and the denigration of labor. Alienation is successfully resisted where there is either access to the power needed to change the evaluation or a will to generate that power.

Dorothee Soelle has another insight into why we have so often embraced so many mistaken forms of dominion. She does not locate this in the fall from grace but in an inner emptiness that invariably sets people on a hunt for fullness without dealing with their emptiness. "Only by confronting the nothingness inside ourselves can we aspire to a new act of creation."[17] This is an important point. Every time a human being enters the world, creation begins in a way all over again. There is a formless void, although it is usually not experienced before adolescence. This emptiness can be filled during the course of a lifetime if it is read accurately. The void can be filled if there is a personal sensitivity about the nature of one's real needs. These needs are not for power or comforts or gain, as they are so often misread. They are for meaning and love, things that require a real interiority to perceive and attain. An outward journey that does not go inward will leave the void unfilled. In fact, it can become a yawning chasm. Efforts at dominion that are not rooted in truth about one's person or are out of touch with one's own interiority inevitably try to complete one's own creation in aberrant ways.

In his famous book *The Denial of Death*, Ernest Becker touches what I believe is the deepest source of the propensity to confuse dominion and domination. As others have also observed, he sees that fear of death as the mainspring of many of our actions.[18] It is the worm at the core of life's project, as William James would contend. The way we most often deal with this fear is by repressing it, but, as with every other repressed fear or desire, it resurfaces. The drive for heroism is the affect and in turn the concept that Freud recognized and Becker focuses on to explain how this fear of death resurfaces.

This is a very important clue for our understanding of how the commission to dominion is interpreted once death enters the scene through sin. It would explain much about conquest and ruthless competition and many of the larger-than-life antics we read of daily in the business world. Predators ever on the look out for a "quick killing" or a lucrative acquisition, like all other would-be conquistadors, are striving for a manmade immortality. Dominion under God in obedience to God's command is not part of their myth, but it is still part of their psyche because this commission from God is a call that all people have deep in their being. The predator's way of handling this call is to revert to psychological ploys to repress the fear of death, followed by aspirations for projects or actions of heroic stature. Those who are unaware of the call to dominion, those who are out of touch with themselves, often attempt to measure up to the challenge coming from their fear by overinvesting themselves in work.

In this chapter we have looked at creation and the commission to dominion. We have also seen how often domination and alienation characterize the situations we find ourselves in. Where do we go from here? Creation is one of two main interventions of Yahweh on behalf of his people. Exodus complements the creation event. Exodus is necessary to free the creation event to do its thing. Yahweh's intervention in Egypt frees the dominated who are alienated. It also frees the dominators. Yahweh did not leave those whom He had created alone to live out the consequences of their Fall from grace. As the human drama moved east of Eden, God pursued the protagonists. In time, the God of Abraham, Isaac, and Jacob decided on a new creation through liberation—hence, the Exodus.

The condition of the workers in Egypt was dire:

> Taskmasters were set over the Israelites to oppress them with forced labor. Thus they had to build for Pharaoh. . . . [They were reduced] to cruel slavery, making life bitter with hard work in mortar and brick and all kinds of field work—the whole cruel fate of slaves. (Exod. 1:11–14)

Yahweh hears the cry of the Israelites and decides to bring them into a land where work is easy because the people would be free and the land would be bountiful. The Lord tells Moses:

> I have witnessed the affliction of my people in Egypt and have heard their cry of complaint against their slave drivers . . . [I will] lead them out of that land into a good and spacious land, a land flowing with milk and honey . . . (Exod. 3:7–8)

Exodus is the wider horizon against which this whole drama of alienation and dominion should be seen. One of the reasons for saying this is that the creation story came fairly late to Israel. The Genesis account was composed long after the Book of Exodus and its description of Yahweh's mighty deed in freeing the Hebrew slaves from the tyranny of Egypt.[19] Israel experienced Yahweh first as the God who liberates. The idea of the God who created the world out of nothing was subsequent to and ancillary to this Exodus event.

The Exodus is germane because every successful exercise of dominion, every victory over alienation, is a liberation of God's people and a resumption of the created order Yahweh intends for his people.

Those who return to dominion after succumbing either to alienation or domination—dominion's two misfires—are actualizing the Exodus event anew. They are, in fact, participating in both of the primary interventions of God, the creation and the Exodus. These interventions of God's power are still going on. But now they require human agency to become actual. They are no longer unilateral events. They await the invitation and consent of Adam and Eve's progeny.

In this chapter we have dealt almost exclusively with the anthropology latent in the Genesis account. When the reader ponders or prays over these, he or she can begin to see the different self-image, God image, and work understandings these considerations contain. We have worked according to our own understanding of work's place in our lives. It is important that that understanding correspond to God's revelation (insofar as this is ever possible) because our work is making us who we are. It is also making the world what it is. We are not only making a living by work, work is making the persons we are and the life we live—for better or for worse.

# 3
# Work and Rest

Before we leave the creation myth, we must look closely at the seventh day since it is of great significance for how we see and go about our daily work. The theme examined in the present chapter should be especially pertinent to those who are very involved in their work either because they enjoy it, or because they have to be, or because they tend to be workaholics.

Recall this classic text:

> Since on the seventh day God was finished with the work He had been doing, He rested on the seventh day from all the work He had undertaken. So God blessed the seventh day and made it holy, because on it He rested from all the work he had done in creation. (Gen. 2:2–3)

There was something special that was created on the seventh day. It was *manucha*, rest![1] God created a day with this special ingredient in it not because God was tired but because God knew we would be tired from the responsibilities of taking dominion over creation during the other six days of the week. The seventh day is for us and it has something as essential for humanity as the other six days' creations of water and light, fish and birds, land and vegetation.

Without the seventh day's gift of rest, efforts at dominion will become disordered. Unlike all other things created for our use, the right use of the seventh day requires a reversal of dominion. We don't take dominion over it. This rest has to be entered. It cannot be used, exploited, bent, or manipulated. It can only be acceded to. Reflections on the sabbath by rabbis and Jewish scholars (most notably Abraham Joshua Heschel) are helpful for insight into the sabbath and for ways of celebrating it (though they do not focus on its great value for a spirituality of work).

The sabbath, Heschel notes, is a structure embedded not in space but in time.[2] It moves along as time moves. Every seventh day it can be entered as if it were a cathedral. It is already blessed by God with God's own inner quality of holiness. God made this day holy so that God's people could be made whole by a regular observance of its obligations. These were reducible to two. One was to welcome the sabbath at sundown on Friday, making room for her as if she were a queen or a bride.[3] The other obligation was to observe its stipulations, principally by refraining from work.

Not working, however, is just the precondition for receiving the many blessings of the sabbath. Yahweh used this day to form Israel like no other day in the week. On it Israel learned how to let God come and provide for her so she could see how God had provided for her the previous six days. Every sabbath Israel appreciated anew how God had filled the earth with all the things that God had pronounced as good. Observant Jews could come to see more fully on the sabbath what was true of all the things their hands had worked with all week, namely, that they were the work of God's hands.

The sabbath was the day in which those who took on the responsibilities of dominion six days a week were invited to reclaim their childhood before God, something always true but not easily internalized while they were trying to exercise dominion over things. Workers had to learn to play again and enjoy being cared for as children.

Adulthood is a curse if it can't be part of an interplay with childhood. Dominion as a responsibility becomes too heavy if it is the only commission we know. The sabbath is its complementary commission: "Remember to keep holy the Sabbath day" (Deut. 5:12). The sabbath mediates the holiness of God to us. Sabbath time is time for learning to be use-less. It is a time for learning to let God speak to us through creation as we forgo the pursuit of our own purposes so that God's agenda can be known and done by us and through us.

Another thing we know about God's sabbath agenda is that it is meant to be a delight to us:

> If you hold back your foot on the sabbath from following your own purposes on my holy day, if you call the sabbath a delight and the Lord's holy day honorable; if you honor it by not following your ways, seeking your interests, then I promise you you shall delight in me. And I will make you ride on the heights of the earth. And I will nourish you with the heritage of Jacob your father. (Isa. 58:13–14)

The desires of the human heart are for God and for more than God. Or, better, for finding God in the things we use, see, and experience. While there were no "musts" on the sabbath, many things were allowed. Sabbath, consequently, was an unbusy time for leisure and learning, friendship and solitude, community and silence, worship and play. It was a day in which God could touch the many desires of the heart.

The sabbath is a paradox. It is a day that requires great discipline to do nothing. Our efforts are focused on letting our guard down so that God can get to us. The reason we aren't given dominion over the seventh day is so that we can learn to let God achieve dominion over us. It is a day for learning how to hope and who to hope in. An inability to conform to this habit of the sabbath may indicate that one's hopes are rooted in one's work rather than in God. Working seven days a week ensures that we will forget whose hands have made what we work with and whose hands accompany every part of our work. To exercise the kind of dominion that befits creatures, we must recognize that this day is the dialectical opposite of the other six days. One day a week God must have dominion over us.

Although his book does not comment explicitly on keeping the sabbath, Joseph Pieper's *Leisure: The Basis of Culture* has things to say about leisure that illumine the meaning of this seventh day of rest. Leisure is a form of silence, he contends, the purpose of which is to be able to wonder, to savor, to apprehend life as a whole and myself as a part of that whole.[4] Leisure is its own reason for being. It is not simply a break between periods of work. Its purpose is not to enable one to function better when one returns to work (although it should have that effect). The antithesis of leisure is the need to intervene, to control, to use, to know in order to use. But these are actions and functions of dominion.

Much more destructive of the gift of sabbath, however, is what I

would call near-miss or counterfeit sabbaths. These fall short of the
purposes of this day. They lull us into assuming we know what
sabbaths are, thus lowering our expectations about the delight they
are to be. Counterfeit, near-miss sabbaths are days of dissipation or
distraction from work. A day of rest and rest in God differs notably
from a day filled with diversions and distractions. Our own culture
uses the Christian sabbath, Sunday, to seduce us into confusing real
and counterfeit sabbaths. Think, for example, of the size of the
Sunday newspaper, the omnipresent sports on Sunday television,
and the other entertainments that pervade the seventh day of the
week. Whatever promises to be financially successful inevitably
constitutes a strong force in our economically fueled culture. Once
the so-called blue laws lost their authority to command the comings
and goings, the openings and the closings, on this day, the superficiality of our sabbaths while these laws were in effect was laid bare.
Consequently, our Sundays are just as pell-mell and busy as the
other six days, even though different kinds of activities fill them.

The church, which should be part of the solution and the main
proponent of observing the holiness on the sabbath day, can be part
of the problem. Unpeaceful, rushed, busy worship services cele-
brated by harried, busy, unquiet worship leaders are not good
witnesses to the importance of the day. They make the faithful
assume that this is the most we can hope for from the sabbath. And
when the churches have to cram their entire week's agenda into
Sunday, the delight God means us to enjoy on this day becomes
remote.

For some it is easier to use the text of the Scriptures rather than
reflections on a theme of Scripture. There are two particular passages that can help in understanding the sabbath. One of these
already cited, Genesis 2:1–3, provides the felicitous image of God
resting on the seventh day. Those who keep the sabbath participate
in the rest of this resting God. But the God who rests also saw that
all that was made was good. On this day, therefore we savor with the
Creator the deep-down goodness of all the created things that surround us. We can also savor the fact that we are one with all of this
creation, being ourselves created. Communion with nature, consequently, is praiseworthy for at least part of the sabbath day. In a
word, the sabbath keeper who rests with the God who rests on the

seventh day imitates God in whose image and likeness he or she was made.

A second text that is pregnant with meaning for this theme of rest is the sixteenth chapter of Exodus. Its context is significant. Israel has fled Egypt and the oppression of its taskmasters. The promise of her own land, a land flowing with milk and honey, seemed to recede as the dire discomforts of the desert began to overwhelm the people. They grumble against Moses and Aaron and begin to recall with hankering the "fleshpots" they knew back in Egypt. Yahweh answers Moses' prayer with the gift of manna and the institution of the sabbath:

> Morning after morning they gathered it till they had enough to eat; but when the sun grew hot, the manna melted away. On the sixth day they gathered twice as much food. . . . [Moses told them,] "That is what the Lord prescribed. Tomorrow is a day of complete rest, the sabbath, sacred to the Lord. . . . Take note! The Lord has given you the sabbath. That is why on the sixth day he gives you food for two days. On the seventh day everyone is to stay home and no one is to go out." After that the people rested on the seventh day. (Exod. 16:21–30)

Before the Ten Commandments were given on Sinai, the sabbath is prescribed. Before there is Israel the place, there is Israel the disgruntled mob of sojourners whom Yahweh means to shape into a people. The sabbath, evidently, was meant to play a big part in their formation as a people.

The sabbath formed the young Jesus, as it formed all observant, faithful Jewish children and adults. During his public ministry Jesus had many surprising things to say about the sabbath. At the same time, his behavior on the sabbath outraged those who were Israel's religious authorities at the time.

An ascending Christology sees Jesus coming into his maturity and self-understanding the way everyone else does, gradually and by means of all the helps and ills that flesh is heir to.[5] If, as Christians have customarily surmised, Jesus began his public ministry around the age of thirty, he would have already experienced more than fifteen hundred sabbath observances. When he went down to

Nazareth as an infant, he wasn't subject only to Mary and Joseph. He was also subject to the Law, to the synagogue, and to the observance of the religious customs of his family and village. And, notably, he was subject to the sabbath as the most important day in the Jewish week.

As did every devout Jew, Jesus learned through the sabbath. The rabbis used to describe the sabbath as the day when "another breath" was breathed into the observant during the course of the day.[6] It was a breath from another world, the world from which this world had come, and from the world to come. Before he imparted the breath of God to his disciples on the first day of his risen life, Jesus had spent a lifetime taking in this other breath from the realm of God. He had placed no obstacles on the breath of the Spirit of God in him. "He does not ration his gift of the Spirit" (John 3:34).

In the years of his hidden life, Jesus learned how to let God have his way with him. At least we can infer from his ministry that this is what had happened in the quiet of his heart during his hidden years. He obviously learned, because he unrelentingly taught that we could trust God. The dramatic core experience of the sabbaths Jesus and his mother and for some time his father spent together, was to know God's rest. But the effect of that weekly experience was formation in trust. In the final analysis, the purpose of the sabbath is the formation of a people in trust of God. By entering into God's rest with regularity, one learns how to trust God and entrust oneself to God.

Jesus' public ministry was a living out loud of what he had lived quietly before that. Sabbath was a time for people to let God be God to them, to let God father them and mother them. But this was the way Jesus acted on the sabbath during his public ministry. His disciples quized him: When you approach the mystery of God, what do you say? What do we say? Say, "Our Father . . . ," he taught them. God was never more father and mother to the devout Jew than on the sabbath. The sabbath wasn't for those who had their act together but for those who needed God to heal and sustain them and make them whole again.

The God Jesus trusted was compassionate far beyond what Judaism had dreamed or imagined. It would have been hard to come to know the compassion of God on the sabbath through the twisted contortions of Israel's professional religious class. Like self-appointed referees for God they spent that day blowing their whistles constantly about who was out of bounds, who was in bounds, who should be penalized, and who should be awarded for their sabbath performances.

The ordinary people, of course, did not feel they could presume to interpret the mind of God about sabbath observance, so there was also a power thing going on. The people had been maneuvered into feeling beholden to the religious professionals for their knowledge about what was to be done or not done on this day. The lore that had to be known about the sabbath was presented as an exquisitely intricate set of instructions that were virtually inaccessible to everyone other than the members of the elite groups who were in on the secrets.[7] But this knowledge had to be made known lest the easily displeased (according to the professionals) God were to be offended. The pharisaical elite had turned the purpose of the sabbath inside out. They made people feel that they had to be righteous for the sabbath. But the sabbath had been instituted for people to be touched by the holiness of God. With no little impatience, Jesus righted the order by insisting, "The sabbath was made for man not man for the sabbath" (Mark 2:27).

Much of the eventually fatal tension between Jesus and the professionals erupted over their very different interpretations of the sabbath. Jesus acted freely on the sabbath and the professionals felt threatened by his example. His observance frequently bent the rules when an act of compassion was called for. When one of the key players on the field plays by rules other than those imposed by the referees, something has to give. It did. They removed him from the field in order to get on with their game, their threatened authority now reasserted.

Jesus did not flaunt the Law of course, including the law of the sabbath. He did, however, distinguish between the customs that had grown up around the law of the sabbath and that law's real intent. He accused the pharisees in this as in other things of "making a fine art of setting aside God's commandment in the interests of keeping your traditions" (Mark 7:9). The deepest error was that they had come to view righteousness as something they could acquire through good works rather than as something God would bestow upon them through or independently of their good works. A system of meritocracy had subtly supplanted the reign of compassion and care God intended Israel to know and experience.

There seems to have been a quantum leap in the middle of Jesus' ministry with respect to the sabbath. The first stage saw him observing the sabbath yet acting freely about it because he had seen such bondage to the letter of the law in the manner of its observance. In the second stage he did a surprising thing, he began to subsume the sabbath into himself.

He did not abrogate the law of sabbath any more than he abrogated anything else in the sacred tradition of the Judaism he so loved and revered. In this as in so much else, Jesus functioned like the figure of Moses leading the people out of the enslavement to law to which they had succumbed. He seemed to have less patience with an incompassionate interpretation of how to live the sabbath than with any of the Pharisee's other misinterpretations. For example, when he and his hungry disciples were criticized by the Pharisees for plucking ears of corn on the sabbath, he recalled for his critics the text that exclaims, "It is mercy I desire and not sacrifice" (Matt. 12:7).

The letter of the sabbath was observance. The spirit of sabbath was neither observance nor righteousness, but growth in trust of a God who is compassion without limit. Consequently, when someone was in need on the sabbath, Jesus' responses flew in the face of the sabbath stipulations that had quantified and confined God's righteousness. He had breathed in the other breath and, therefore, the spirit of the law whose letter he freely disobeyed when God's compassion prompted him to.

"The Son of Man is indeed Lord of the sabbath" (Matt. 12:8). Some exegetes believe this is an editorial insertion added to the text after Jesus' resurrection and ascension, when a very young Christianity was separating itself from Judaism.[8] Maybe so. The need to apologize for so advanced a claim during his public ministry is unnecessary. During his ministry he began to see the very strong hold over the people exercised by the law of sabbath and the authorities who refereed its observance. He simply and clearly sought to lead the people into freedom from this bondage.

Moreover, "the Son of Man" is the one who is called the Lord of the sabbath. This figure has been the subject of much research. Jesus used it of himself but his hearers seemed not to catch the nuance in his doing so. The title derives from a very late apocryphal tradition, especially from the books of Ezra and Daniel. In the first of these there is an obscure figure of suffering and humility.[9] In the second there is a messianic figure who is wrapped in glory.[10] Since his discplies didn't understand the humiliation that awaited him Jesus used this title presumably to enable them to put together these seemingly irreconcilable characteristics after his death and resurrection. It is not impossible, therefore, for the statement to have come from the lips of Jesus during his ministry, though the full meaning of it could not have penetrated until this new Moses extricated himself from the unfree Egypt that Judaism had made for itself. He still had a Red Sea to cross before they would be able to reconcile the shame and the glory that came upon this Son of Man.

The real bombshell Jesus delivered about the sabbath was not about his freedom from the neurotic constraints to which it had been subjected. It was, rather, about his own person's relationship to it. The key text in this matter reads, "Come to me, all you who are weary and find life burdensome, and I will refresh you" (Matt. 11:28) Refresh you or, better, rest you (the verb used here is *anapauō*, which means "to give rest"). This new Moses found that he couldn't simply set people free from the Law, which had become a bondage, without their attaching themselves to him. But this developed into his responding to their need to find a place of rest by making himself that place. Thus, he became the one who brought them into the rest of God. He was the door they entered. He was the sabbath's Lord, in contrast to the master the Pharisees had tried to make themselves. This is not an abrogation of the law of sabbath but a subsumption of it into himself. This is quite a leap in Christology. Come to me and you will find what you had sought in the sabbath but didn't find! Come to me and you will enter the rest of God! Just who does he think he is? was the inevitable reaction.

Before trying to answer this question, remember that it gets more complicated, as the passage continues: "Take my yoke upon your shoulders and learn from me, for I am gentle and humble of heart. Your souls will find rest, for my yoke is easy and my burden light" (Matt. 11:29–30). In the same breath in which he invites them into a new locus of rest, he saddles them with a yoke. Although it is packaged in the best light he can give it, it's still a yoke. What is this yoke and how can it improve on what they had known before?

The rabbis used the metaphor of a yoke to describe the Mosaic Law. In interpreting it they had amassed six hundred thirteen commandments for the people to know and obey. This often had the effect of quantifying God in the minds of the people. When the people failed to measure up to the huge quantities of good works they were expected to do, their failure alienated them affectively from this quantified God while they remained dependent on the religious leadership to retain their relationship to God. Not only does this preposterous Jesus challenge this doubly disfigured God image and self-image, but he subsumes both the sabbath and the Law unto himself.

How did he come to such a self-understanding? If we understand Jesus' consciousness developmentally, with an ascending Christology, then it seems right to trace Jesus' self-understanding to his experience of the sabbaths themselves. They were the weekly days of communion with God, who had so much to teach this young Nazarene about himself, his relationship with God, and God's relationship to Israel.

During Jesus' public ministry, great developments took place in his understanding of God and himself and Israel. It is enlightening, for example, to examine the context in which Jesus makes the outlandish claims of his relationship to the sabbath and the Law. The context in which he claims to be Lord of the sabbath involves a corn-plucking incident when the Pharisees complain about the freedom of Jesus' disciples. Immediately before that we read, "Father, Lord of heaven and earth, I offer you praise; for what you have hidden from the learned and the clever you have revealed to the merest children" (Matt. 1:25). The children here include Jesus himself, who never ceased being a child and a special child at that, as he learned in the course of all the sabbaths he had lived through. What did he learn? "That everything has been given over to me by my Father. No one knows the Son but the Father, and no one knows the Father but the Son—and anyone to whom the Son wishes to reveal him" (Matt. 11:27). To know God as father is to know the spirit at the heart of the Law. And it is to know the whole Law. But Jesus not only knows the heart and the whole of the Law; he also knows that the Law, wonder of wonders, has been given over to him. That is why he was so presumptuous as to subsume the sabbath and Law into himself. It wasn't his idea. The Law became his to administer: no one could know the Law now except him, who knew the Father.

The text at this point focuses on work. An invitation to come to him is extended to all "you who labor and are heavy burdened" (Matt. 11:28).[11] If we fit that description, we must ask what it is Jesus might provide us with and how our work would change if we accepted the invitation.

If we were to find our rest in him, surely that would be a clear advantage over finding it in a particular day of the week. But what Jesus is claiming here is that he is becoming the structure of rest and holiness that had made the sabbath day special for Israel. Consequently, where the person of Jesus is, there that holiness is. If one has access to him, one can come into the rest that Israel sought and be touched by the holiness of God at the same time. He removed the sabbath from the time frame in which it was enclosed.

He could do so because he had come into a relationship with God and God's holiness hitherto unknown and even unimagined in Israel. With his death and resurrection he could become an abiding presence in the lives of his followers since he was no longer confined to a space and a time. "Anyone who loves me will be true to my word, and my Father will love him; we will come to him and make our dwelling place with him" (John 14:23). The risen Jesus broke not only the time frame of the sabbath, he also broke the space frame of worship. As he told the Samaritan woman, "an hour is coming when you will worship the Father neither on this mountain nor in Jerusalem" (John 4:21).

A follower of Christ does not have to wait for sundown on Friday to enter the "cathedral in time" that is the sabbath. One need only enter one's inner space, there to find the one who would be the sabbath for him or her. Jesus can bring us into the rest of God. He who is seated at the right hand of the Father is also seated in the inner sanctum of the heart, which his love has made a dwelling place for him and his Father in the Spirit. It is no longer the day that is

holy. It is the follower whom love makes holy. Jesus makes the heart
a sanctum, a holy place, a place of refreshment with God's holiness.

It seemed significant enough to the inspired New Testament
writer to have Jesus not only rise from the dead but be seated at the
right hand of the Father. Why seated? Because the Father was
seated. Why was the Father seated? Because the work of the Father
in the six days of creation was in a sense completed. And the
complementary work of the Son, the redemption he accomplished,
was also in a sense completed with his resurrecton. What remains to
be done now is for those who believe these things to avail themselves of the infinite riches of the completed work of the Father and
the Son. Believers are the work God hasn't completed. God's work is
completed by their appropriation of the redemption and the co-
creation of the creation in the Spirit through the Son for the Father.

The life of grace that we carry around in our earthen vessels as a
treasure is not bound to space or time. We do not have to leave the
rest of God that we have in Christ to go to work. That center goes
where we go, is where we are, and is accessible to us at all times.
This is the marvel of the promise of rest that Jesus made and that his
death and resurrection make possible. This rest is neither time
intensive nor space intensive. It is there with each entry into the
cathedral carved out by God in the sanctum of the believer's heart.

The condition for finding rest in the person of Jesus is that we take
his yoke upon our shoulders (which is where yokes go) and learn
from him—even more specifically, from his heart. To enter his rest,
one has to enter the way to him. His way and his person are
inextricably linked. Both are to be found in the yoke that is the
Gospel. Rest, then, comes in degrees and over time as we learn from
him and his heart. Rest so often eluded those burdened down by the
yoke of the Law. Not only did they have to work but they had to work
themselves into redemption. The burden of the Law misinterpreted
made redemption something to be acquired and won rather than, as
with the Christian, something to be believed and rested in because
it is already in place.

The idea that rest is entered by learning the path to it is not
original with Jesus. Jeremiah also taught about the path that would
lead to rest: "Stand beside the earliest roads, ask the pathways of old

which is the way to good and walk in it; thus you will find rest for your souls" (Jer. 6:16). But Jesus is even more concrete. He claims that he can be known and that his qualities can be perceived by those who come to him. Two of his most helpful qualities for learning how to rest were identified when he said, "I am gentle and humble of heart" (Matt. 11:29). His gentleness must have been evident, judging by the ease with which everyone approaches him—children, beggars, the poor, women, sinners. And the humility of Jesus is also evident, especially in the manner in which he comports himself in his final days. We come to know the humility of this man beginning with his majestic entry into Jerusalem—"Your king comes to you without display astride an ass, astride a colt, the foal of a beast of burden" (Matt. 21:5)—all the way through his terrible suffering, during which "he opened not his mouth." The strong, meek way in which he bore the yoke placed on his shoulders by his Father is stunning evidence of his character. From the beginning to the end, he emptied himself for others and for God.

Can we enter the rest without the yoke? One way of answering that question is to reflect on our own experience of what makes it hard to find rest. What most often makes us restless is a disordered relationship to something or someone in our lives. One of the functions of the yoke of the Gospel is to enable us to live in a relationship of order and integrity with people and things who are part of our lives. Obedience to this yoke of the Gospel teaches us the way to order and integrity. Obedience to the Gospel is identical with learning from the gentle and humble Jesus. If we would have the rest of God that Jesus can mediate we need to know the Gospel. The Gospel is both a yoke and a path. Obedience to it brings rest.

There is a pregnant passage in the Epistle to the Hebrews that spells out in clear terms this relationship between yoke and rest, and the restlessness that results from a lack of receptivity to it. The passage begins with a quote from Psalm 95: "If today you should hear his voice harden not your hearts as at the revolt . . . I was angered with that generation . . . [and] I swore in my anger, they shall never enter into my rest" (Heb. 3:7–11)

Entering into the rest of God can be ultimate and eternal. It can also be proximate and for now. Hearing the voice or word of God is the key to this rest, whether it is for today or for eternity. This voice of God or word of God can either be heard and not believed—"the word they heard did not profit them, for they did not receive it in faith" (Heb. 4:2)—or a person can be too hard hearted even to hear it in the first place.

Hardened hearts are often too busy working or too busy thinking or too taken up with their sin. The effect is the same, namely, being out of touch with or closed in one's heart. God could speak to such hearts every day but they might never hear the word. When a person who is too busy to hear God is supposedly working for God, this condition is particularly pathetic. When, as frequently happens, a person does hear the voice or word of God but has found a counterfeit place of rest and chooses not to reexamine it lest it be lost, he or she is in the rest that sin furnishes and chooses not to be disturbed.

Another scenario occurs when a person hears and believes the word and takes it in. When this is the case, Hebrews has a helpfully graphic passage about the power of the word that has been given room. "The word of God is living and effective, sharper than any two-edged sword. It penetrates and divides soul and spirit, joints and marrow; it judges the thoughts and reflections of the heart" (Heb. 4:12). The word cuts into all of the attachments and arrange- ments, the rationalizations and relationships, that make for rest- lessness or hardness of heart. If the word is successful in its reception and penetration, the roots of the restlessness can be severed and God's rest can be enjoyed. The passage ends with a reminder: "Nothing is concealed from him; all lies bare and exposed to the eyes of him to whom we must render an account" (Heb. 4:13).

We are used to seeking our rest in things and people, comforts and arrangements, not in the rest of God. To get from the former condition to the latter we need to be attentive to the nudges, the "words," by which God would lead us into that which alone will satisfy. The author of Hebrews notes that "the promise of entrance into his rest still holds" (Heb. 4:1). He is certain that "a sabbath rest still remains for the people of God. And he who enters into God's rest, rests from his own work as God did from his" (Heb. 4:10).

A brief comment on the development from the Jewish sabbath to the Christian Sunday is in order. There are obscurities, of course, as with everything historical that didn't receive a clear mandate from Jesus. The fact that Jesus rose from the dead on the first day of the week and the fact that he had mandated a meal for his followers in his memory (eventually called Eucharist) conspired to displace the old sabbath day with the new Day of the Lord, which we call Sunday. Those who believed in Jesus, and who were no longer under the strictures of the Law or the authority of the Jews, needed a fixed time to assemble for worship; the choice of a special day of the week was a practical way of meeting this need.

The Emperor Constantine brought the state in on the act by decreeing in A.D. 321 that there was to be one day a week that was to be a day of rest and religious observance. This was to be "the venerable day of the sun."[12] By the fifth century, the same busybody religious prescriptions and proscriptions that had circumscribed the Jewish sabbath began to resurface around the Christian Sunday.[13]

# 4

# The God Who Works

This book is more concerned with providing a methodology than it is with elaborating a theology of work. It presumes that most readers have a religious orientation that can be made operational without having to be corrected to any great extent. This presumption may be less valid with the theme treated in this chapter.

The theme of this chapter is based in the idea that God is no less present in the workplace than in the place of worship. The fact that God is not often experienced in the workplace is not evidence of God's indifference to it or absence from it. Rather, it is a sign of poor religious education and of the superficiality of our discernment. Without an expectation of finding God in the work situation, it's unlikely that God will be found there. The place of work is usually taken to be a worldly or secular kind of place, to which God must be brought by the believer if there is to be anything of God there at all. This doesn't do justice to the omnipresence of God in all created reality. To God, nothing is profane (Acts 10:15).

A spirituality of work that thinks only in terms of bringing one's sense of God to work will inevitably become patronizing. If one learns to find God at work, one's spirituality will be nurtured and strengthened there. God can be mediated to the worker through colleagues, objectives of the work, materials worked with, interactions between workers, and other circumstances of the work site. One's union with God need not grow faint in the workplace as though God were absent. Rather, one's union with God can be strengthened when God is found there.

A considerable amount of theology is needed to validate these contentions. The reader will be spared this validation since our intent is not to teach theology but to assist the reader in making his or her faith operational. To this end, two exemplary people who managed to find God acting in everyday things will be discussed.

## Ignatius Loyola

Saint Ignatius Loyola learned to find God in the everyday things that he had once experienced as merely pedestrian and devoid of any spiritual dimension. He left enough of a legacy in written spiritual counsels to enable others to learn how to attain to the same experience of God. We will concentrate on only one of the counsels found in the last meditation of his Spiritual Exercises.

The person who undertakes these exercises is instructed in the third point of the final meditation to "consider how God works and labors for me in all creatures . . . He conducts Himself as one who labors. . . ."[1] In the previous point the person was to have reflected on "how God dwells in all creatures . . . in the elements, animals, plants, oneself." In the first point the person was to have reflected on all the blessings of creation and redemption plus the special favors received from God.

These three points for reflection are preceded by a petition asking God to grant us the grace to come to "an intimate knowledge of the many blessings received" so that, realizing how bountiful God has been to me, "I may in all things love and serve the Divine Majesty."[2] Without the gift of this grace one would not be able to see the reality of God bestowing these special favors while at the same time indwelling all the things that circumscribe our lives. With that grace, however, anything and everything can prove sacramental, a medium through which God pushes through to us in some way.

What is distinctive about Ignatius's insight is not just the emphasis on the sacramental character of all created things for those who seek and receive the grace to see this. It is the insight into the manner in which God is present. "He conducts Himself as one who labors."[3] This means not only that God is indwelling all of the things God made but also that God is actively working in them. Even more beautiful for one who has been given the eyes to see this, God has a motive in working, namely, God is working *for me*. Ignatius suggests that the one praying try to come to this insight. Not, of course, that

God is working exclusively for me, he assures the one praying. What is exclusive is the gift of grace to see the truth that God is working for me even though it is equally true that God is working for many. In fact, God is working in all things for all of us.

Ignatius instructed trainees in the Jesuit order that when they were in the midst of their studies of philosophy or theology they were to shorten the time they had spent in prayer as novices and seek the presence of God in the midst of their studies. He instructed their supriors to give them guidance

> in seeking the presence of our Lord in all things, as for example in conversing with someone, in walking, looking, tasting, hearing, understanding, and in all that they do since it is true that His Divine Majesty is in all things by His presence, power, and essence.[4]

Note here that Ignatius indicates that God can be found not occasionally but in *all* things. The Spiritual Exercises begin with a vision of all things as means God has provided for us to come to the end for which God made us. So nothing is neutral if one becomes convinced that this view of things is true.

Ignatius goes on to contrast favorably this way of finding God in things with formal prayer and meditation. Finding God in the everyday things we do is "much easier than raising oneself to divine things that are more abstract and which require more effort to make them present to ourselves."[5]

Ignatius indicated that this finding God in the course of one's daily work could be strengthened by a frequent offering of one's work to God. This constantly purified the intention one had in undertaking the work in the first place. The Jesuit scholastics were taught to

> exercise themselves by frequently offering to God our Lord their studies and the effort they demand, seeing that they have undertaken them for His love to the sacrifice of personal tastes, so that to some extent at least we may be of service to His Divine Majesty by helping souls for whom He died.[6]

If the intentions one has for working are directed to God, this will go a long way in helping one find God in the work one does.

There is reason to believe that the frequency and depth of one's work intentionality will elicit a strong response from God. This was certainly Ignatius's own experience. He comments:

> the more one binds himself to God our Lord and shows himself more generous towards his Divine Majesty, the more he will find God more generous towards himself and the more disposed will he be to receive graces and spiritual gifts which are greater every day.[7]

The limitless generosity of God will show itself before, during, and after work if one's intentionality is to find God in what one does.

Ignatius had a specific term for when he succeeded in discovering God in things and situations. He called it devotion. In his autobiography, which is narrated in the third person, he describes his growth in union with God in the years after his conversion experience.

> He [Ignatius] had always been growing in devotion, that is, in the facility to find God. And now [during his writing of the Jesuit Constitutions, toward the end of his life] this was the case, more than any other time of his entire life. And every time and hour that he wished to find God, he found Him.[8]

Devotion was the measure of spiritual growth. For Ignatius, this meant a developing facility in finding God. He saw devotion as having different levels of intensity. Sometimes it was simply a sense of God's presence, more a believing than a feeling. At other times there was more affectivity. And sometimes there was such a strong sense of God's presence that tears would flow.

Of all God's creatures the human being is the one in whom God's presence and working is easiest to discern. Growth in devotion to God could develop, Ignatius assured his brothers in the Society of Jesus, if each of them were to revere their colleagues "in such a manner that by observing one another, they grow in devotion and the praise of God our Lord, whom each one should endeavor to recognize as in His image."[9] We can presume that God is present to and working in the human person more fully than in any other creature. So Ignatius's advice about learning the practice by first seeking to find God in people is good advice, especially for beginners. Imagine how spiritually nurturing our work would be if we pierced through to the transcendent dignity and importance in God's eyes of the colleagues with whom we work regularly. Each of them could become an *eikon* ("image") of God, unless their flaws were too distracting. But an image has to be pretty flawed before it ceases to be a stand-in for God's presence to us. It is also possible that the flaws are not in the image but in the eye of the beholder. The "interests" of the beholder can obscure, even obliterate, the image of God, the God who is to be beheld in the other. Jealousy, envy, anger, fear, competition, or any other faults or vices can block the possibility of finding God in the beheld.

The God Ignatius found was God at work, and at work for him, no less. Finding God's will was contingent on finding God. Ignatius saw the purpose of the Spiritual Exercises as finding God's will for one's life. But after one came to understand the particular state of life one is called into, it is still necessary to know in an ongoing way the particulars of God's will as one's vocation is lived out. This ongoing will can be discovered in an ongoing way when one finds God in the things that surround one's work, especially when devotion accompanies this finding.

The rule Ignatius wrote for Jesuits emphasizes the key condition for success in finding God in things. Believers

> should be often exhorted to seek God Our Lord in all things, stripping off from themselves an [autonomous] love of creatures—to the extent that this is possible—in order to turn their love [of them] upon the Creator of them, by loving Him in all creatures and all of them in Him. [10]

As Michael Buckley comments:

> The way one finds God is to find things the way they are. They do not exist in themselves; they exist only in God. Conversely, if one is going to love God, one must love Him the way he is—namely, in all things. [11]

The last point of the meditation that has framed our brief discussion of Ignatius indicates how far this finding God in all things can bring those who have the grace to come to this vision and experience of God at work in the world. (And recall we are talking about a grace, not an exercise in mental gymnastics. Recall, too, that the way one relates to this is to ask, seek, and knock on the door if one wishes to be given such a grace.) All the previous points in the prayer have had a person looking up from below, so to speak, through creatures. In this last point a continuum between God and creatures is glimpsed in their common qualities, which begin in God.

> Consider all blessings and gifts as descending from above. Thus my limited power comes from the supreme and infinite power above and so, too, justice, goodness, mercy, etc. descend from above as the rays of light descend from the sun, and the waters flow from their fountains. . . .[12]

The special qualities found in people, things, circumstances, and even oneself can bring one up Jacob's ladder, so to speak, to their origin or font, and back down the ladder, to their embodiments. The qualities that are common to God and the human order can now be seen as a continuum that descends from above.

Ignatius did not speculate about the providence of God, which is the theological subject closest to this theme of finding God at work in our world. Instead, Ignatius saw that the providence of God was, for all practical purposes, embodied in the person of Christ. God had handed dominion and the governance of the world over to him. To follow Christ with devotion dispensed with the need for speculation about divine providence. By learning a few simple methods people were able to find the God they sought in Christ. They committed themselves to following him and his will for them. They found his will insofar as they found God in the everyday things they did. Ignatius saw the laboring Christ as the one who issues a call to follow him in his labors so that we may follow him in glory.

## Jesus

Jesus' life is also a model for finding God at work in one's work situation. In fact, Jesus' insight into God at work seems to have been the basis for his ministry. Jesus ascribed the actions he undertook in his own ministry to his insight into the work he saw God doing in the circumstances in which he found himself. "My Father is at work until now, and I am at work as well" (John 5:17). The occasion for this remark was the curing of a man on the sabbath. The Jews objected to his having done so, and he answered them with the claim that his action was linked to what he saw "My Father" doing. He responded by talking about what he saw God doing and its relationship to his own actions: "I solemnly assure you, the Son cannot do anything by himself—he can do only what he sees the Father doing. For whatever the Father does, the Son does likewise" (John 5:19).

In several places in John's Gospel, Jesus uses a suggestive metaphor to indicate the effect on his person of finding God at work in the people he meets. It is like food for him. Take, for example, his long soul-probing conversation with the Samaritan woman. As the text indicates, he had arrived tired at the well, but after the dialogue he is so refreshed that he is not in need of the food the disciples fetched from town for him while he was conversing. God's working in her became clear to Jesus. As she made herself vulnerable to him he discovered that God had been working furiously in her. She departs with the return of the disciples. A dialogue then ensues: "Rabbi, eat something." But he told them, "I have food to eat of which you do not know." At this the disciples asked one another, "Do you suppose that someone has brought him something to eat?" Jesus explained to them, "Doing the will of him who sent me and bringing his work to completion is my food" (John 4:31–34). This is a commentary on the impact the woman at the well had on Jesus. The discovery of God's working in persons was food to him, as it can be for any follower of Christ, especially if that discovery is accompanied by a sense that one is being used as an instrument of God to complete his work.

There is another passage that compares the experience of finding God at work in other people with receiving food for one's soul. In this second situation, however, it is the Son of Man who gives the food. He tells the crowd that sought him out after the multiplication of the loaves, "You should not be working for perishable food but for food that remains unto life eternal, food which the Son of Man will give you; it is on him that God the Father has set his seal" (John 6:27).

As with Ignatius so also here, the question of work's intentionality is raised. Working for perishable food is working myopically, merely for the sake of work or for the food one can put on the table as a result of work. It is a here-today-gone-tomorrow undertaking, without any further dimension to it. But to work for food that lasts gives work a transcendent meaning. For work to have this further dimension, however, personal intentionality must be linked to Jesus, who will somehow be this food. In the context of John 6, this food is probably first of all the Eucharist. But everything in John has more than one meaning. If we look further, it becomes evident that this food that the Son of Man will give to one whose work intentionality transcends the here and now repeats what Jesus experienced when he made himself instrumental in completing his Father's work. The best commentary on the idea in John 6:27, about working for food that lasts, is, therefore, John 4:33, about the food Jesus experienced by doing his Father's work. But instead of the Father being the food and supplying the meaning of the work, the Son does. He would make himself the food that nourishes the soul of the follower of Christ. What does it mean that this food lasts? It means that the bond that is forged between Christ and ourselves as his instruments, and the ministerial action that results, have some kind of permanence. (We will inquire more deeply about this in chapter 6.)

The passage goes on: "At this they said to him, 'What must we do to perform the works of God?' Jesus replied, 'This is the work of God: have faith in the One whom he sent'" (John 6:28–29). Jesus' listeners had understood "works that last" as works that God somehow does. But Jesus accepts their way of putting it and answers them by saying that the work of God is twofold—he himself is the work of God and their faith in him is the work of God. If they want to do the works God would accomplish through them they must first believe in him with the faith God gives them. The chief work God would accomplish is to bring all to belief in him so that all can know the Son whom the Father sent. This is not God's only work, but it is God's chief work.

In the episode with the Samaritan woman there is another rich

image of finding and cooperating with God's work. After citing a
proverb to introduce the image of the harvest, Jesus tells the disciples who had unsuccessfully sought to give him food, "Open your
eyes and see! The fields are shining for the harvest! The reaper
already collects his wages and gathers a yield for eternal life, that
sower and reaper may rejoice together" (John 4:35–36). The sower
is God and the reapers are those who have discerned what has been
planted by God in the fields (in hearts). Significant here is a division
of labor, with the different moments of planting, growing, and
reaping, and the different instrumentalities that are needed for
God's work to be completed. If a reaper doesn't come along, the
harvest goes to waste. If the reaper doesn't see when the harvest is
shining, white, and ready, the crop is wasted. The reaping fails when
it is either premature or overdue. If the reaper appears on time and
takes the necessary action when a yield for eternal life is ready, the
sower and reaper will rejoice together since doing their respective
tasks has produced the one sought-for result. But even before this
final rejoicing, the reaper is described as having reason to rejoice
because he is collecting wages even now as he works. The wage he
receives is this food that lasts for eternal life, or, in Ignatius's terms,
the devotion that brings such consolation of heart in the present life.

## Finding Wisdom

Jesus' way of finding God was not wholly original. It had precedents. We can find those precedents in faithful Israel. One precedent was in Israel's use of memory. Another was in her wisdom
tradition.

It seems obvious that God became present to Israel through
discernible interventions in the course of her history, interventions
that lived on in her memory. But once these interventions, like the
Exodus, were over, they did not simply become history. They had
not started off in the human order but originated outside of time, so
to speak, in the mind and heart of God. These events entered time
through hearts, believing hearts. They shaped these hearts. These
interventions (eventually called moments of *kairos*, or "sacred
time," because they have their origins in God, as distinct from

moments of *chronos,* or "clock time," which originate in the created
world) were not bound by past, present, and future. *Kairos* moments could be retrieved, therefore, and they were meant to be, so
that their impact and formative value would continue on in the
present in those who retrieved them.

The Jewish liturgical year (as also the Christian liturgical year) is
built on the assumption that past *kairos* moments can become
present and can have a powerful impact in the hearts of the cele-
brants. This recalling is not simply a function of memory. If it were,
*karois* events would fade into *chronos:* they would be treated as
history and recalled as past time without any expectation that they
could have a present impact on the commemorators.

Memory, therefore, was a key faculty of spiritual growth in Israel.
This is no less true of Jesus. If we wish to take his humanity seriously
we have to take his human consciousness seriously. If we do, we can
see that his spirituality and spiritual growth developed in the same
way any devout Jew's spirituality developed, namely, through the
*kairos* moments. Through these Israel came to know what she
meant to God and what she was to do as chosen by God.

Israel's liturgical year would have sensitized and formed the young
Jesus to God's ways even before he could name God as his Father
and himself as Son. Consequently, Jesus became aware of the daily
evidence of God's presence in the world first and foremost by being
a faithful participant in the liturgical life of Judaism, the chief
element of which was the weekly sabbath, as we have already seen.
If one were faithful in celebrating with one's synagogue God's great
interventions—the *kairos* moments that made Israel what she was—
one would also become sensitive to the many daily and personal
ways in which God's presence can be discerned. The liturgical year
and the celebrative memory participants bring to it is still the most
formative influence on Jewish and Christian spirituality.

The wisdom tradition of Israel offers other precedents for Jesus'
way of finding God in ordinary life. This tradition had two stages.
The first of these is embodied in the Psalms. The Psalmist delighted
in the presence of God that penetrated the world and spoke through it.

"The heavens declare the glory of God and the whole firmament
proclaims his handiwork. Day pours out the word to day and night to

night imparts knowledge; not a word nor a discourse whose voice is
not heard; through all the earth their voice resounds and to the ends
of the earth, their message. (Ps. 19:2–5) Let all your works give you
thanks, O Lord, and let your faithful ones bless you. Let them
discourse of the glory of your kingdom and speak of your might." (Ps.
145:9–11)

Devout Israel was familiar with the doctrine that God was present to
and could be discerned in created things. Things bespoke God's
presence to them. No! Even more strongly, they proclaimed God
and manifested God's attributes and glory. The immanence of the
divine in creatures was affirmed, notwithstanding Israel's very
strong emphasis on the transcendence of God.

The need to align these two seemingly contradictory affirma-
tions—the transcendent otherness of God versus the immanent
presence of God in creatures—was one of the reasons for the development of a second stage of the wisdom tradition. There are two
interesting components in this later development: one is the figure
of Wisdom: the other is the ethical content of what was mediated by
this Wisdom.

First, who or what is the peculiar figure called Wisdom? It was not
itself a creature since it antedated creation; nor was it God:

> The Lord begot me, the firstborn of his ways, the forerunner of his
> prodigies of long ago; from of old I was poured forth, at the first before
> the earth. . . . When he set for the sea its limit, so that the waters
> should not transgress his command; then was I beside him as his
> craftsman and I was his delight day by day, playing before him all the
> while, playing on the surface of his earth and I found delight in the
> sons of men." (Prov. 8:22–31)

As the reader can see, Wisdom is personlike and creaturelike but
also unlike persons and creatures. Wisdom was in on the founding of
the earth (Prov. 3:19). "How manifold are your works, O Lord! in
wisdom you have wrought them all" (Ps. 104:24). This wisdom,
which somehow is in each creature, also calls out from them and
from the situations creatures are in. "Creation not only exists, it also
discharges truth."[13]

> Wisdom cries aloud in the street, in the open squares she raises her voice; down the crowded ways she calls out, at the city gates she utters her words: "How long, you simple ones, will you love inanity?" (Prov. 1:20–22)

Inanity is preferred when Wisdom's call is not heard or heeded.

The second part of this late development is the peculiar content that is learned when Wisdom's call is heeded. What is learned when Wisdom teaches is an order that preexists the learner. That order is found in what God had made; it is immanent in and mediated by creatures. It addresses its hearers as to how they are to treat what God has made and how they are to act in an ethical way in the world God has created. If a person seeks out this wisdom in the created order, he or she

> will understand the fear of the Lord; the knowledge of the Lord you will find; . . . you will understand rectitude and justice, honesty, every good path; for wisdom will enter your heart, knowledge will please your soul, discretion will watch over you, understanding will guard you. (Prov. 2:5–11)

The fruit of this discovered, uncovered wisdom "is better than gold, yes, than pure gold" (Prov. 8:19). In fact, so valuable is Wisdom that "he who finds me finds life" (Prov. 8:35).

Jesus was privy to this wisdom tradition and to its manner of coming to truth. The fact that Jesus' way of finding God was not original with him should be a source of comfort to us because there is always the suspicion that we can never measure up to his way of relating to God. But if the ways in which God can be found were effective for generations before Jesus, then they will be available and accessible to us now.

And no less a source of comfort for us should be the fact that the wisdom tradition was subsumed by and in the person of Jesus in much the same way as the sabbath was. Paul calls him the wisdom of God (1 Cor. 1:24). He is also called our wisdom (1 Cor. 1:30). In the second chapter of First Corinthians, Paul indicates that the wisdom he himself communicated to the Corinthians was Christ crucified (1 Cor. 2:1–2). The contents of this wisdom of God was Jesus as a person in the present as well as in the Gospel story.

Paul was certainly aware of the doctrine of the self-revelation of God through creation. In fact, he clearly affirmed it. "Since the creation of the world, invisible realities, God's eternal power and divinity, have become visible, recognized through the things he has made" (Rom. 1:20). Notwithstanding his awareness of the doctrine, Paul saw the supreme manifestation of the wisdom of God not in creation but in Jesus and the Gospel. It was still evident in creation but it was more evident, for Paul, in Jesus and him crucified. Nor was the figure of wisdom a wraithlike being hiding in created things.

Upon reflection the church would soon connect this peculiar figure who preceded creation with the Second Person of the Blessed Trinity. The Gospels, furthermore, revealed an order in creation that conveyed an order for communal and personal life that had never been divined by even the most devout of Jews. Jesus called people to follow him into that kind of order.

## Making God's Interests Ours

So far we have the testimony of Israel and Jesus as well as Ignatius to assure us that God is present in the world and can be found there with regularity. It remains now to be more specific about the ways in which this God can be found where we work. Insofar as we have success in doing so, we will succeed in our attempt to develop a spirituality of work.

We will be more able to see the workings of God in our lives and in our work if we are more aware of the interests of God. All of God's revelation could be distilled to what we might term a double interest: God's actions in time and history are "interested" actions, interested, namely, to love and be loved. There seem to be three principal ways God has of pursuing this double interest. The first way is to create. But this first way is not exhausted by a once-and-for-all act of creating. God's relationship with all creatures is such that there is also an ongoing activity of providing what is needed by the creature to continue on in existence, sustaining itself or realizing its potential according to its particular nature. The second way God pursues this interest is by the activity of redemption, winning back that which is lost. The third way God has of pursuing this interest is to make it possible for things and structures to be perfected so that they function for the ends for which they were established. We will now explain these three ways in more detail.

The creative, creational activity of God is evident in plants and birds, sun and water, minerals and air, and so forth. But to be more specific, all the materials that go into making what we produce as workers rely, if not directly then ultimately, on the creative hand of God. Even the materials of the second creation, meaning what we have made from these raw materials, can be seen as coming from God mediated by human ingenuity. Beyond what we ourselves do and make, think of all the things we rely on, all that we need sustained in existence in order to do our work.

Jesus, for example, could see the birds feeding themselves and yet ascribe their sustenance to God's act of feeding them. And the robes with which the wild flowers were wrapped he ascribed to an action of the Divine Clothier. Christians must learn to see as Jesus saw in this matter of the work of God going on all around us. This contention holds notwithstanding our modern knowledge of such things as photosynthesis and instinctual behavior that give partial explanations for the activities of plants and birds mentioned here. If William Blake could see the hand of God in the fearful symmetry of the tiger burning bright in the forests of the night surely the Christian can learn from and yet see beyond scientific explanations to the activity of God at work in their world.

Our sophisticated knowledge would have been acquired at too high a price if we were to forget what the rest of creation knows. Job's comments are pertinent here:

> Ask the beasts to teach you, and the birds of the air to tell you; Or the reptiles of the earth to instruct you, and the fish of the sea to inform you. Which of all these does not know that the hand of God has done this? That in his hand is the soul of every living thing. (Job 12:7–10)

Just the fact of their own gift of life, as also the lives of their colleagues, is an even better reason for workers to pause and see a creating, sustaining, and providing God at work in their midst. Never to have appreciated life as a gift beyond our own making is to completely miss what God has done in creating human beings.

Once the creative, providential activity of God has been perceived, it can be met with reverence and awe, thanksgiving and praise. Any or all of these are appropriate responses. Inappropriate is a dullness of mind and heart that takes everything for granted and fails to see anything transcendent in the here and now of our everyday rounds.

A second mode of divine activity in people is redemptive. God is ever about the task of calling back into union and reconciliation all of us who are always at some distance due to moral failings, disbelief, or spiritual tepidity. God's redemptive actions surface in human consciousness in many different forms: in dissatisfaction with one's life, for example; or in a sudden jolt, like the loss of a job or the death of a loved one, that forces one to face what hasn't been faced; or in pricks of conscience, discovery of another's unfaithfulness, or just plain emptiness. Any or all of these, or a myriad of less dramatic possibilities, can sensitize us to the activity of God in us, pursuing his interest in our redemption. One might not at first detect the action of God at such moments, but after the fact we often see how certain events brought about a fuller turning toward God. Whatever it is that begins the journey back into union and peace with God, there are usually several stages in God's action, after the initial one, which is often experienced as compunction. These stages might take the form of empowerment to pray; to repent; to seek counsel, forgiveness, absolution, or reconciliation with and forgiveness from wronged parties. All of these are initiated in the person by God, whose passionate interest is union with the one who is made to be in union with God.

The God whom Jesus knew was never satisfied until the unrepentant sinner turned away from sin and faced anew the rejoicing, forgiving Father. Those who themselves have known God's mercy will be able to assist others to discover the process of repentance at work in themselves. By having a sensitivity to the movements of God in oneself or others, one can assist this primary interest of God in the work of redemption in the world. This kind of assistance would have to be handled delicately since proselytizing or fundamentalist intrusions into another person's privacy would be resisted in most work situations. The point, however, is that the Sower needs reapers who are ready, willing, and able to do the job. The reaper helps to convince potential penitents to discover the actions of God in them in order to come to peace and reconciliation with God.

The third kind of activity of God in history and in time is sublational. I borrow this term from philosophy. A sublational action is one that elevates something, drawing it out of deficiency, immaturity, or disunion into a greater perfection, maturity, or union. Applied to God working in and through us, sublational actions would be those which are targeted to perfect what is humanly, socially, or structurally imperfect. Created reality is scripted to come to fullness. One form of that fullness is transcendent, through redemption. Another form of that fullness is immanent, through sublation.

"God's glory is man fully alive," according to an oft-quoted adage first voiced by Iranaeus.[14] But "man" fully alive is a creature of both time and eternity, an achievement in the course of history as well as a victory of grace living with eternal life. More specifically, "man" fully alive is a social being who interacts with the world and others in a complex and ever changing series of structures. Perfecting these interactions and the structures that express them is part of the sublational action of God.

The theological warrant for creating this third category comes from twentieth-century theology in general and Vatican II specifically. Sublation refers to the idea that Christ's intention was "to restore the temporal sphere of things and to develop it unceasingly."[15] Christ's intention was "to perfect the temporal order in its own intrinsic strength and excellence" through the structures people have made to organize themselves and pursue their purposes. "Man" fully alive refers to something more than individuals. It refers to the social wholes of which he is a part. Neither God nor we ourselves can prescind from these wholes that make or break individual persons.

One can begin to see the enormous implications behind this category of sublation. If it is true that God is highly interested in perfecting the human order in its this-worldly conditions, and therefore, that we will find God acting on people in terms of this interest, then we should be primed to expect God's nudges in us concerning all those things that have to do with perfecting our social structures and systems, particularly those operating in our work situations.

God's agenda is much greater than "the salvation of souls." His agenda is the perfecting of all that is human. This fuller agenda is not of less interest to God than the salvation of souls. Come to think of it, these are not two agendas, but one. We distinguish these only to enlarge our understanding of what God is about in us and our world. If we saw God as interested only in saving our souls we would be in serious error. A Christianity that "is so heavenly minded that it is of no earthly good" is either immature or insincere. The nicest thing we could say about such an attitude is that it is on its way to becoming Christianity.

To be more specific, God's sublational action in us nudges us to value certain kinds of behavior in the workplace: honesty, harmony, productivity, efficiency, justice, and creativity, to name a few. If a work situation has workers who prize these qualities and act on the basis of this esteem, then the sublational actions of God in the hearts of the workers are bearing fruit. The result will be systems and structures that come even closer to realizing their potential. These structures and systems are "goods of order" that make the pursuit of valid human goods and purposes easier to attain.[16] If the purposes or goods pursued are valid, the perfecting of the structures (or their establishment, if such is necessary) is part of the sublation process.

It is not a matter of indifference to God that the result of our work and that of the whole enterprise at which we work is the human good, the good of humanity. God is interested in bringing the humanity that we have as gift singly and collectively to its fullness as humanity. If this is true then human labor, our work, would have to be at the core of this interest of God since so many of the best and worst things that happen to humanity happen through or at the work site. It is there that we express ourselves, come to be who we are, and at the same time give shape to the human order. It is also at work that some of the greatest disorder and denigration of humanity takes place.

## In the Employ Of

One scriptural theme that conveys all the essential qualities of the God who works for us is *covenant*. Covenant is the warmest theme in Scripture. Covenant is unabashedly, unmistakably an intimacy-seeking initiative of God, hard as that might be to believe. The fact is it wasn't believed, even after a number of tries from God's side. The final, new covenant "in my blood" says better than words how seriously God takes covenant and the lengths he will go to achieve it.

The achievement of covenant requires that the party to whom the pact is extended accept God's initiative and ratify it. The consequence is a mutuality of accepted behavior to be undertaken or avoided in light of the covenant. In covenants made between peoples, multiple covenants are possible. But with the covenant made by God to a people, only one covenant is possible.

These things being so, it should be obvious that being in a covenant shapes a world view, a lens, on self, God, and one's relationship to the people with whom God has covenanted. Covenant, therefore, makes serious demands on the understanding one has about the work one does. To put it graphically: before you ever take a salaried position, while you are in a salaried position, and after you relinquish your salaried position, you were, are, and will not cease to be in the employ of the God who has covenanted with the people of which you are a part. This Employer works by means of subcontractors, one of whom is your human boss. Your Employer is for you in a way the most beneficent boss there could ever be. Unlike a human boss, your Employer is constantly at work for you. He is so much more than an employer that the title never even made it into the list of God's honorific titles. Nonetheless he is your Employer, and he has interests that he pursues in and through the work you do and the work that is done by your colleagues, plant, corporation, and industry.

To be in his employ wins you a whole range of perks and benefits that he wants you to enjoy. One of these is freedom. Not freedom from work but freedom from fears incited by work. Some of these would be fear of your boss, fear of being fired, fear of being disapproved of or rejected by coworkers, fear of failure in business.

This freedom isn't automatic with entry into God's covenant, but the fact that there is a covenant relationship is a guarantee that this freedom can be developed. The opportunity for it comes with the establishment of the covenant. The conversion from fear to freedom

is symbolized by the Exodus of the Israelites from the bondage of
the taskmasters to the land that promised and delivered flowing milk
and abundant honey. But this path or way or road must be traveled
by everyone who enters into covenant. With this covenant, God
supplies us the power to undertake the journey he calls us to. The
actual walk cannot be undertaken by the Employer. But we can—
and, to be successful, must—take the journey accompanied by the
Employer. Those who do not undertake it will experience the same
fears as those outside the covenant.

The same can be said of joy and peace, and, while we're at it, all
the other fruits of the Spirit. These are love, patient endurance,
kindness, generosity, faith, mildness, and chastity (Gal. 5:22).
These are benefits, powers, and virtues personally experienced by
those with whom God has covenanted through Christ in the Spirit.
In no case is the power lacking to one who chooses to use it. To be
brought into covenant is to be brought into a series of powers. To
disbelieve this or to be ignorant of this insures that the powers will
never come to the fore.

The experience of those who follow Christ is not always one of
covenant as such. It is more often an experience of "being led." He
leads them out of and back into the world that he and the Father so
loved that his Father sent him and he came. The place in which
followers of Christ find themselves most frequently is at work, where
the business of production or service is carried out.

It would be invaluable for one's spirituality if one not only had
experience of being led by God in Christ but experienced being led
by him in the world of work. Otherwise one works only because of
exigency or because of a desire unrelated to the experience of
Christ.

The purpose of this chapter has been to create an expectation and
to suggest ways of finding God in one's work experience, even if one
has not yet felt led to it. Again, we find an instructive example in
Ignatius's Spiritual Exercises. Ignatius has the retreatants imagine
themselves called by a king who has launched a major campaign and
is seeking companions so that he can complete what he has begun.
The call comes from a king who is so immersed in the campaign that
he is undergoing all its vicissitudes personally. The follower must be
content to share the lot of the king, which at present is an ordeal.

The follower is called "to work with me by day, and watch with me by night, etc., that as he has had a share in the toil with me, afterwards, he may share in the victory with me."[17] Ignatius then has the retreatants envision this same situation, but now hear the call as coming from Christ who has launched the campaign. Christ is imagined to say, "Whoever wishes to join me in this enterprise must be willing to labor with me, that by following me in suffering, he may follow me in glory."[18]

God is at work in the world in and through Christ. God's interests have been made known to us through the Son. The Son is interested in having us join him in completing the work the Father sent him to accomplish. His labor for us is then complemented by our labor for him. This is the covenant made operational. The call to labor with and for him is not a call to leave the world and join the ranks of clergy or religous—at least it doesn't often mean that. It means to be at work in the world with an eye on and looking out for God's interests and purposes. We find these in the course of working and make them our own. And we find him who would have us for his own.

# 5

# Evil at Work

Most people experience more of a sense of God's absence than of his presence at the workplace. No one works in a utopia. Varying degrees of dissatisfaction are operative in every job. Dissatisfaction can be due to individuals—bosses, managers, owners, or colleagues. Or it can be with the job arrangement, the structures, the system.

This chapter will focus on all these types of job dissatisfaction, but it will do so in terms that are more theological than moral. If we were to focus on the morality of the workplace, we would deal with work-related sins, like greed and sloth, selfishness and dishonesty, sexual harassment and ruthless competition, backbiting and padding expense accounts. Here we will not deal with any of these moral failings, important as they are, because they ordinarily do not require a lot of reflection. Instead, they usually need a more insistent conscience or a change of will, heart, and motivation. Theological reflection, however, enables us to probe areas that are deeper and more complex, namely, the structural elements that exacerbate the moral failings of employees.

Several general questions are worth asking at the outset of any theological reflection on our work: Who benefits from this enterprise and who loses? What spirit moves this whole effort? What does our work do to us? These questions prompt a recollection of the most general of all principles about work, namely, that people are its purpose. This simple principle, however, needs to be fleshed out.

People create themselves through their actions in a way that no other creature in creation does. The bird building a nest and a snail creeping toward food are acting according to their natures. They cannot do otherwise. When humans act, however, they are not ordinarily acting according to something necessitated by nature. If there is even a modicum of freedom in what they do, they are choosing to make themselves who they are by what they do. They gather up the effects of past choices and actions and carry them with them into their becoming. As we make our way we make ourselves. One of the main actions we undertake is the act of working. Work is one of the things that makes us who we are. Work is a major way we have of fulfilling ourselves, of making us more who we choose to be. Unfortunately, it is too frequently the unmaking of many.

The difference between work making us humanly more or making us humanly less is the difference between good work and bad work, as Schumacher calls it. Work is bad when the physical, relational, or psychological conditions within which it is done are degrading or debilitating or defeating. It is bad when the compensation for it is unjust or exploitative. It is bad when the degree of actual participation is not in keeping with the workers' dignity as choosing, thinking creatures. If people make themselves by their work, they must have a say in the work they do and how they do it.

Good work, on the other hand, is work that is undertaken within a context in which there is "the definite conviction of the primacy of the person over things and of human labor over capital."[1] More specifically, good work happens only when the purpose of property, capital, and ownership are remembered.

> Property is acquired first of all through work in order that it may serve work. . . . The means of production cannot be possessed against labor, they cannot be possessed for possession's sake, because the only legitimate title to their possession is that they should serve labor.[2]

Josef Tischner, who was one of the theoreticians behind the Polish labor initiative Solidarity as well as its chaplain during the first years of its heroic struggle, described good work as "a conversation in the service of life."[3] This is a felicitous turn of phrase. Conversation requires a two-way street; work, then, would be the fruit of reciprocity. The reciprocity would be between owner and manager, owner and worker, worker and manager, worker and worker, capital and labor, human resources and material resources, need and response, supply and demand, possibility and necessity. If the conversation takes place in the service of life it will be life giving, both for those who work and for those who are served by their work. Toil, by way of contrast, is not life giving for those who do it, nor should it be for those who are its beneficiaries.

## Economism

What makes work bad? Many things, obviously; people, invariably. Many would say, "the system" or "the bottom line." When this supposed insight is countered by the undeniable fact that without a bottom line or a system no business can survive, the conversation stops. The problem is not with the bottom line as such. It has many possible thresholds. When bottom-line considerations are scaled so high that people considerations are ignored, then the problem is the bottom line. In such cases, the problem is one of economism.

Economism, I would contend, is the real culprit behind most bad work.[4] It is the deepest source of evil in many workplaces. Its impact pervades the world of work, from the macroeconomic level to local situations. Although few workers have ever heard of economism, everyone who has been an employee has felt its destructive power.

Economism is a logic whose irrationality is seldom exposed. It is a mind-set that conceals a radical inconsistency. It is a culture that devalues the very things we profess to stand for. It is a disease of the spirit that unmakes everyone touched by it.

The logic of economism is based on the assumption that where there is demand, there will be supply. So far, so good. When the demand is for goods and services, suppliers will be found. When the demand comes from those in need of goods and services basic to their human well-being, economism responds by saying that these needs will be supplied only if they are paid for. There is a logic here. But what if those with the needs can't pay for them? This is where economism begins to show its true colors. Economic considerations are allowed to function like a court passing sentence on human needs, denying clemency for those who cannot pay and giving a hearing to those who can or to those who can make a profit while meeting these needs. Economism, then, is on the bench and the people in the dock. There is a logic here but it is perverted. Economism specializes in knowing the price of everything and the value of nothing. Its blindest spot is the value of persons. It functions in a way that denies the economy exists for people. It affirms the opposite: people exist for the economy.

Economism is a mind-set that manipulates the notion of what is real in such a way that it is able to accept some workplace claims and deny others as unrealistic. This mind-set too readily reduces the irreducible transcendental dignity of persons to the measure of their productivity, efficiency, profitability, and competitiveness. Of course, the worker should be required to be productive, and so forth. But economism's mind-set makes these the only qualities to be taken into account. Any other quality or claim is largely beside the point. When a more wholistic view of personhood is called for and claims are made on the basis of this, they are consigned to the cold gray world of the "unrealistic." Since economism operates with a circumscribed version of "reality," any fuller version of our humanity, with the change in demands that attend this fuller version, is disparaged as inviable.

This is still very abstract, but becomes terrifyingly concrete when a fuller account of personhood comes up against the bottom line of economism. In some ways, the bottom line is a synonym for this mind-set. But, as we have already seen, the problem is not with the bottom line as such but with how it is administered. If management make its threshold low enough so that people considerations can be taken into account, managers and owners cannot be accused of economism. Human considerations are never tidy; they are always unique and unpredictable: A child's sickness, divorce, religious holidays, flextime, day care—the list of human considerations is endless. Interrelating people's needs and economic considerations is what makes management an art. If both are factored into management's decisions then economism is not the mind-set of the managers. But if the bottom line is the only standard used and people are reduced to mere ciphers, then economism is alive and well at the workplace and with the management in question. Where economism holds court, money talks and obeisant mutes do its bidding.

When economism enters into a culture, it makes it over. This is true of corporate cultures, local cultures, and national cultures. Edgar Schein, the reigning analyst of corporate cultures, describes them as follows: corporate cultures are

> the basic assumptions and beliefs that are shared by members of an organization . . . [they] operate unconsciously and define in a basic taken-for granted fashion an organization's view of itself and its environment.[5]

These assumptions and beliefs are learned responses that if conformed to make possible a culture's internal integration.

Soon after joining a company, a worker knows whether its culture is one in which economism rules, even though the notion of a corporate culture and the term *economism* may be unfamiliar to him or her. If both the bottom line and people are factored into the company's style of operating, the corporate culture is not one of economism. If concern for the bottom line is so great that economic considerations are primary in every decision, then economism has succeeded in winning still another outpost in its campaign to conquer the world.

We need not be abstract about the success economism has had in penetrating our national culture. Our stated beliefs are noble but our everyday operational practices are usually out of synch with these beliefs. Examples of this abound: in this morning's newspaper I see stories about poor rural health care; the millions of Americans who are without health insurance because they cannot afford it; teachers' salaries contrasted with the salaries of celebrity athletes. I notice the grandiose conditions of the places that house our deposits contrasted with the places our working poor have to live in, and the millions of dollars culled from a firm by a corporate raider who never worked there contrasted to a worker who worked there all his life only to lose his livelihood after the raider has siphoned off the assets. We who claim to believe in liberty and justice for all are so used to things being this way that we no longer see their absurdity. Economism has numbed our perceptions. It allows us to give lip service to values while practices that contradict them proliferate. It even supplies us with rationalizations to explain away these contradictions, and to label those who lament our situation as malcontents or losers who can't measure up in the real world.

Finally, economism is a disease of the spirit. It is ever ready to hand over the "object" of infinite worth for thirty pieces of silver. While avowing noble beliefs, it in fact values capital over people, gain over relationships, accumulation over community, solvency over integrity. The disease does not discriminate: it afflicts both those who have and those who simply want to have, both laborer and executive, white collar and blue collar, capitalist and socialist. Most of its carriers go undetected since their split consciousness allows them to profess one thing and do another.

The sickness is not in the economy but in the human spirit. When it is more blatant and breaks out in the form of greed or avarice or cheating, it comes closer to being remedied because it can be seen for what it is. It usually isn't blatant. Consequently, its most successful carriers do not see themselves as diseased; they live with it happily and dispense its deadly wisdom to all and sundry while the symptoms of the disease go undetected.

I first discovered the term *economism* in the papal encyclical *On Human Work*. In that encyclical, the pope claims that "the error of economism considers human labor solely according to its economic purpose."[6] It usually

> includes a conviction of the primacy and superiority of the material and directly or indirectly places the spiritual and the personal [man's activity, moral values, and such matters] in a position of subordination to material reality.[7]

We cannot blame the modern development of the science of economics for the emergence of economism, since economism was alive and well long before that. But economics certainly doesn't help matters, since from its inception it has implicitly embraced an individualistic conception of society.[8] So much of economic theory, from Adam Smith on, has gone far to advance a justification for this unacknowledged mind-set of economism by claiming that the pursuit by individuals and aggregates of individuals of their own self-interests would result in maximum material welfare for everyone else through some miraculous "unintended accidental consequence."[9] While the science of economics has grown much more sophisticated since its early days, it seems that most of its theorists have not yet overcome the individualistic perspective of its early days. Be that as it may, the fact is that economism is alive and well, economics or no.

## Benign and Demonic Spirits

If economism is a disease of the spirit that can afflict both individuals and collectivities like corporations or nations, it is natural to ask how theology's knowledge of the world of spirits can enlighten us on the subject.

A recent trenchant analysis of angels, demons, and what the ancients saw in them, can bring new depth to our understanding of modern economism. The ancients believed in angels, demons, principalities, spirits, and such like because they experienced such powers operating between and among themselves. They knew these intermediate powers were not God, although they experienced their influence over humans and their affairs. Walter Wink, a professor of biblical interpretation at Auburn Theological Seminary in New York City, has analyzed these principalities and power, demons and gods, angels and devils.[10] He has discovered that they had an inner ethos with an outer manifestation. His analyses have been able to distinguish what our forebearers saw as one and named in an effort to exercise some influence over them. Interestingly enough, current management and business literature as well as political science are trying to feel their respective ways into the very matters that have long been scorned by moderns, namely, the unseen but highly influential world of the culture, or spirit, of an organization, corporation, or nation. The world of angels and the world of corporate cultures aren't as far apart as we imagined.

Any new insight into a nation's or organization's spirit must surely be worth exploring since the nations of the twentieth century are accountable for the deaths of about one hundred million people. Looking at the behaviors of nations or groups in terms of the inner spiritual dynamics moving in them was old hat to the ancients but is still virgin territory to us.

There are two reasons for the novelty of this optic on the world of spirits and their dynamics. For one, we moderns tend to be so individualistic that we are unused to viewing corporate entities— whether organizations or industries or nations—as anything more than aggregates of individuals. The idea that these corporate entities might be moved by "spirits" is preposterous to most of us. It smacks of fundamentalism. In addition, our endemic materialism, not to mention a general scorn for a world view that makes room for angels and demons, does not make a line of thinking such as Wink's easy to accept. The fact is that Wink is saying something cogent, something we have already examined in a different light; his thesis does not require us to revert to the ancients' world view.

His argument runs along these lines. There is a communality between the ancients' experience of evil and our own. We can come to appreciate the wisdom they had in construing these symbolic projections as they did. They had to explain evil, overwhelming evil, in such a way that the world and their own existence in it made sense. So do we. One has to judge whether our own explanations explain evil better or handle it better than theirs did. By believing in and naming these intermediate powers as they did, powers which were at the same time under God's dominion, they were able to make sense of human existence. The process also empowered them in some slight way to exert some influence on that spirit world, and thus to feel that they were not mere objects moved about by the whim of these powers, some of which were benign, some of which were destructive.

The ancients were not imagining the evil that at times threatened to engulf them. It was really there and it still is. One difference between now and then is that "the demonic in our own time has a peculiar proclivity for institutional structures."[11] Evil tends to have incarnated itself in structures and ways of operating. Again Wink's comment is relevant. The "angels of the nations" (which was one ancient classification of these intermediate beings) can no longer be seen as being "out there" or "up there," according to Wink.[12] Instead, they are the inner ethos animating and sustaining our ways of operating. By "inner ethos" we mean the spirituality that shapes our assumptions and our institutions, allowing us to take some things for granted, others as remediable, and still others as inevitable. This inner ethos, or spirituality, of an organization or nation is a combination of the "benevolent and the demonic."[13]

Recall that early Christians had an active belief in angels, as Jesus also appears to have had. For example, "See that you do not despise one of these little ones, for I say to you that their angels in heaven always look upon the face of my heavenly Father" (Matt. 18:10). Some of the fathers of the church accepted a traditional belief that each nation had an angel. Some even wondered whether the angels of some nations were fallen. Others thought each nation had a good and a bad angel attached to it[14] (see, for example, Rev. 1:4 or 1 Pet. 3:22).

Wink's interest is not in the angels as such but in the inner spiritual quality that becomes flesh and creates the style of thinking and acting in a given institution and community. "Every collective entity that has continuity through time has an angel."[15] The experiential component of this statement certainly needs no proof. We see a special spirit in every school, corporation, church, store, hospital, even nation. Maybe the ancients tired of counting the myriad hosts of angels because they intuited that there were as many angels as there were social entities.

The spirits moving some social entities are adverse to human beings while others are benign. One need not subscribe to belief in angels to accept this statement. What makes one institution assume one spirit rather than another might be explained by the existence of angels, although this would be a very unlikely explanation today. Rather, the important point here is whether the social entity in question (for us, the workplace) enables its people to grow in integrity or whether it is adverse to them. Seeing collectivities as having an inner spirit or spirituality opens up new dimensions in the nature of management. It might even legitimate a more spiritual view of that difficult art. How does a corporation, for example, "exorcise" its demons? Are there any spiritual means available and acceptable to managers and corporations? Are not management consultants frequently asked to perform spiritual direction, healing, or renewal?

If we take our own nation as a case in point, we can see the spiritual tensions that pull at us. At the core of our national ethos, both historically and in terms of our stated self-understanding, has stood the ideal of "freedom and justice for all." We were to develop a bountiful land of opportunity in such a way that all would be its beneficiaries. We were to produce a people who were free to be enterprising and free to choose a way of life and belief as well as a way of making a living. If we have a good angel, that is what the good angel commissions us to be about (or, to put it another way, that's what the good angel is to promote in our hearts). One thing we can be sure of today is that if there is such an angel it must have fallen, or it has yielded its ground to something demonic.

We have a long way to go before there is freedom and justice for all. What we have instead is a national form of economism with all that is implied in this perversion of spirit. The bottom line has never been more important than it is today. The pieties of our nation, which remain an acceptable part of our etiquette, continue to touch our public life but less and less our public policies. The separation of church and state, a wise decision early in the history of our country, has operationally become a separation of economic interests from moral restraints. Our obligation to those who are marginal to our prosperity has never been hazier. Our secularity has tended to free us from the guidance of morality and conscience. The first curtailment of license we the people have been able to agree to in decades is saying no to drugs. In a word, if we have an angel, it is fallen, and it promotes economism as the inner ethos of so much of public life and of so many business situations.

Admitting that his discernment is his alone, Wink believes that the good angel of our nation would lament loudly—if it were given voice—in words such as these:

> wealth is your real god, and all your gravest sins have been committed for it. . . . you demonize Communists because they challenge your system of wealth. Your idolatry is almost unlimited. You are now prepared to blow up the habitable planet for the sake of preserving your freedom to pursue wealth singlemindedly and unencumbered.[16]

Asked why it is so powerless to stop us from going in this direction, the angel replies,

> I can only be what I am: the call to your own fulfillment as a nation. I can, no more than God, revoke your freedom to do evil. If you choose idols, I cannot stop you.[17]

It is not farfetched to claim that each organization has an inner spirit, regardless of how it is explained. When this inner spirit succumbs to the logic of economism it fosters idolatry in the employees who allow themselves to comply with it. If they comply with whatever form its absolutizing of itself and its goals take, they reinforce it, even though they are not conscious of doing so. Economism is largely a concealed logic. It would be much less successful if its logic were exposed. Its subscribers would grow fewer if people realized that "when a demonic institution is functioning normally, it does so by the enthusiastic and willing consent of those it is in the very act of oppressing."[18]

One reason Wink's thesis is so intriguing is because it is a twentieth-century version of a sixteenth-century insight, one that was developed by Saint Ignatius Loyola. Ignatius had a kind of vision of two commanders in chief vying for the allegiance of every person born into time. One of these was Christ, whose strategy was straightforward and was communicated by his followers.[19] This strategy sought to bring people into a freedom from things and desires for things so that one could use what one had as means to ends worthy of one's person. Most of our attachments are not held in that kind of freedom. Hence they mire us rather than serve our purposes. A life free from the bondage of attachments is a consummation devoutly to be wished. That was what Christ's strategy sought to achieve.

The other commander in chief, whose reality was not doubted for a moment by Ignatius, was Satan. His strategy was to lure people into what I have called economism but which Ignatius called "riches."[20] Very often these riches are job related. Even the job itself—retaining it, advancing in it, being recognized for it, and rewarded by it—if these become strong desires this can be a signal that Satan's strategy is succeeding. At least there is reason to think that there is a lack of freedom vis-à-vis the job. From such a seemingly innocuous, even innocent, beginning, the logic of economism can begin to take root. It can become insistent, driving us to try to achieve through "riches" our own autonomy, independence, and a sovereignty that transcends the vulnerability of our humanity. But the self as sovereign is an illusion: the fact is the person sells his or her soul in trying to secure job-related riches that pose as being of great value. And guess who's behind the scenes happily pulling the strings through these desired "riches"? Satan, of course, the commander in chief, whose strategy has once more delivered bound hostages into his camp.

There are endless statistics on those who have lost their jobs or who need a job. There are no statistics on those who have lost their souls while doing the job they do. There is no data to show how many who have been trained and formed in values have entered the job market only to be deformed by conformity to the economism of the plant or corporation. Economism is its own education and formation. In its school, students must unlearn many of the values they once cherished. Angels or no, today's economism is very successful in its vast outreach.

## Self-Interest and Addiction

There are several responses employees can have to economism that prolong it or foment new evils. One of these is to cultivate self-interest. Another is to become a pupil of economism's mind-set. So many become devotees of its logic and addicted to its spirit.

Self-interest can have a negative impact when it operates in a social entity, whether one's place of business or one's nation. Its impact on the spirit of the workers or citizens is bound to be one of looking out for themselves, taking care of themselves and pursuing their own interests. Were self-interest not a factor, there would be a better-than-average chance that workers would be able to invest themselves in the common enterprise with a view to producing something of worth or serving the community by their work. In a word, an organization's economism generates self-interest, or strengthens it if it already exists in the mind-set of the workers. To show concern for others in such a context calls for heroic virtue, an infrequent commodity in the best of circumstances.

The term *self-interest* has meant many things over the centuries, most of them loaded with much emotional freight. Michael Novak has been particularly helpful in pointing out these vastly different meanings. Economists, for example, see self-interested choices as autonomous choices, without purporting to submit them to moral evaluation.[21] This is not the usual meaning of self-interest. Moralists are closer to the ordinary usage when they see self-interested actions as those undertaken in a self-regarding way that disregards adverse effects on others.

Moralists can hardly be blamed for their pessimism. Can anyone doubt that self-interested activity abounds, that it threatens to engulf both public and private life? Hobbes wasn't exactly dreaming when he constructed a whole philosophy on a very dim view of humanity and saw self-interest at every turn. "All society is either for gain or for glory," he observed.[22] We act "not so much for love of our fellows but for love of ourselves."[23] Adam Smith tried to redeem this pessimism by making self-interest the solution rather than the problem everyone thought it was before *The Wealth of Nations*. The concept took still another twist in the early days of this country when the self-interest of the citizenry was expected to act as a check on the powers of the government. James Madison hoped that "the private interest of every individual [would act as] a sentinel over public rights."[24] By and large, however, the general public associates negative connotations to the term notwithstanding the variety of meanings that have been attached to it.

Economism invites self-regard. It shreds whatever community existed before its entry. It cuts into efforts at self-transcendence. It thwarts self-donation. Whatever one's professed values, it dulls them. It disassembles all socially oriented feelings, driving them back into the narrow narcissim of moral pygmies.

Another way of reacting to economism is to become addicted to the stuff. Two organizational consultants, Anne Wilson Schaef and Diane Fassel, have contributed profoundly to our understanding of the factor of addiction in organizations. Addiction is one of the most frequent effects on those who buy into the economism of an organization. They enlist in its service, become infected by its disease, and promote its ersatz wisdom. The only complaint I have about Schaef and Fassel's excellent study is that they don't name the "substance" addicted organizations are addicted to. As is obvious, I believe these addictions are incited by economism. Their explanation of the phenomenon of addiction, however, merits close attention.

Their thesis is that most of the organizations we work for are addicted. These organizations invite addiction, as does the society in which we live.[25] Furthermore, addictive organizations have many of the same characteristics as individual substance abusers. One can become addicted to a substance by ingesting it. One can also become addicted to a process by investing one's selfhood in it.[26] The results are similar: the substance takes over our lives and we find ourselves dependent upon the high we get from it. Its control over us requires that we become dishonest, first to ourselves and then to others, about our personal overinvestment in it. We refuse to surrender our attachment to it even though in the clear light of day we know we would live fuller and healthier lives if we did. Even though we are unhappy about being "hooked" we have grown dependent on what the object of our dependency delivers. The addictive organization invites us to give more and more of our time and talents to it. It eventually requires the investment of our selfhood in its purposes and empty values.

There are several characteristics of an addictive organization that parallel those of the individual addict.[27] Denial of anything, anyone, or any idea that would challenge the addictive situation starts the list. A pervasive confusion is created, so that no one in the operation ever knows exactly what's going on. This leads many employees to spend hours trying to ferret out what's going on or going to go on. This leaves everyone powerless to effect substantial change because the precondition for such change is clear knowledge. Rumors multiply where information is wanting and the workplace thus becomes a rumor mill. Another characteristic is the ever present need for cover-ups in order to present a good front to a gullible or puzzled public. When covering up or lying has been generally accepted, one of the consequences is a numbness in the work force. No one knows exactly what they feel since they can't get a handle on the truth.

Three other characteristics of an organization addicted to economism are even more enlightening. One penchant of such organizations is to operate from a "scarcity model." A scarcity model leads employees to believe that there is only so much to go around, so get what you can while the getting is good.[28] Since the object of the addict's desire is always quantitative, there is never enough of it and need for more is easily incited. More salary, more benefits, more security, more recognition, more perks, more assurance about the future—these are a few of the cravings that are pursued.

Under the impact of economism, as we have seen, there is a gradual surrendering of the more wholistic values and ideals a person may have professed to espouse. Sure enough, the same characteristic that Schaef and Fassel call "ethical deterioration" shows up in addictive organizations. People who get their fix from addictive organizations are willing to ignore their own conscience. Eventually their conscience grows too numb to register its demurs.

Finally, it is characteristic of the addictive organization to be preoccupied with control.[29] There is internal control, control of its employees, control of its piece of the market, control of its shareholders, and control of the image people have about it. These all mirror the condition of the addict whose behavior controls his family and whose family tries to control him. Organization, addict, and family are all under the same illusion, that they will succeed in exercising control.

One of the main features of economism is that it blacks out or denies most of reality in order to exercise control over the thing that is most measureable and quantitative, namely, the world of money and finance. It is an illusory aspiration, of course, and its persistence can only be explained by the addiction of its proponents.

Schaef and Fassel discuss another form of addictive behavior that is work related, namely, workaholism.[30] An employee can become addicted to the organization he or she works for. The reasons for this vary: the mission of the organization can be seductive; loyalty to the company may help one avoid facing one's own emptiness; the organization may offer benefits that over time have created a dependency. But the addictive substance in workaholism is work, pure and simple. Work is where I get my kicks: I become so attached to my work that I am my work, and I have no life apart from it or away from it. The reason it doesn't appear to be the disease it really is is that it is so productive and is seen as valuable to those for whom the work is being performed. Schaef and Fassel make the good point that this kind of behavior is frequently connected with church-related jobs, among others. The supposed nobility of the church's mission hides the actual effects on the person, who loses healthy independence, personal space for spiritual growth, and the poverty of spirit that God needs to teach a person a new agenda.

## Solidarity

The argument as it has developed in this chapter so far needs to be summarized at this point. While bad work has many causes, we have reflected on only one major one, namely, economism. Economism is for all practical purposes a philosophy of life that unfortunately begins and ends in the economy. It is a serious misreading of our humanity, measuring its worth in economic terms. We introduced the question of economism's ultimate source, wondering whether the ideas of angels, demons, or Satan could throw any light on where the inner spirit or ethos of organizations come from or to what they can be traced. This matter was suggestive but not conclusive. Closer to our own experience are the issues of self-interest and addiction, which were seen as the two most frequent reactions to economism.

In this concluding section we will go from evil to good and from the destructive to the constructive. If self-interest and addiction are unfortunate reactions to economism, what would a fortunate reaction be, one that not only refused its blandishments but managed to build something positive in its stead?

Solidarity is the answer, it seems. Although the term itself may be used infrequently, the aspirations behind it are familiar to all of us. Solidarity is a deep aspiration of the human spirit. This aspiration comes from our initial experiences of community or any other form of human wholeness. It is the diametrical opposite of competition, exploitation, and all the other ways self-interested behavior corrupts our hearts and relationships. Solidarity is the antithesis of economism in every meaning of that term. Solidarity is a logic that begins and ends with "us." It is a mind-set that sees things in terms of "our." It is a culture-forming dynamism that is generated by, and at the same time evokes, the deeper values in the human spirit.

As a logic, solidarity can thrive in a situation of supply and demand. Jobs come from supply and demand. Work brings working people together. Solidarity is people together. It comes with effort, and it is maintained with effort. Justice, openness, communication, fairness, and participation are the preconditions for realizing and maintaining solidarity. The place of work can be a source of solidarity second only to the place of worship. Unfortunately, the work-place has more often been a place where adversarialism is learned.

The mind-set of solidarity develops because people thrive in community and wilt when they are at loggerheads with one another. It is confirmed with the growing realization that we are social by nature. Human flourishing happens when and where an individual's gifts are called forth by a community and his or her angularities are smoothed like stones in a stream. Theologians remind us that each person is made in the image and likeness of a God who is trinitarian. Solidarities reflect this radical truth. Individualism disfigures this original image.

There are many counterfeit solidarities. Jesus found himself in one. In counterfeit solidarities, the few benefit themselves at the expense of the many. They claim to be "in this together" with the many, but the game takes place on a playing field made uneven by the few. Jesus' whole ministry could be viewed through an optic of the new solidarity that was to replace a counterfeit one. The Law had become an essential ingredient of the counterfeit—not the Law as such, which was of God, but the use of the Law by those who set themselves up as better than others by inflating their position as interpreters of the Law.

When dignity is violated indignation develops. Indignation can smolder underneath consciousness until it is evoked. Jesus evoked the long-smoldering indignation of his people. They had thought their dignity had to be mediated by the Law and its interpreters. Once they were freed from the bondage of this illusion, a true solidarity grew among them, stoked by indignation and followed by a choice and the grace to forgive those who had held them in bondage. The reign of God on Jesus' lips announced an unmediated dignity, one that was inalienable from persons as persons. Dignity had been meted out to some by a few in a situation of counterfeit solidarity. In the solidarity Jesus tried to establish, human beings didn't mete out dignity to other human beings; rather, they affirmed a dignity that was already there.

The misuse of the Law in Jesus' Israel has parallels in the misuse of the economy today. Take compensation, for example: is not one's sense of self-worth too closely tied to how much money one makes? This error has many subscribers, both among those who receive wages and among those who dole them out. And the parallel becomes even clearer if one thinks in terms of power, especially the power of the money brokers. In our country today, an enormous indignation is growing beneath the surface toward those who decide the fate of workers, communities, and cities without consulting those whose livelihoods depend on the outcome of the decisions.

Solidarity strengthens fragile cultures, whether they be corporate, local, or national. It makes embattled cultures more coherent. Solidarity can become the soul of a culture. Granted, this is infrequent, and even when it does occur, it is only temporary. Regrettably, solidarity lives largely in the realm of aspiration. Economism, by way of contrast, is no one's aspiration and everyone's experience.

What makes for solidarity? A group's experience of indignation, as we have seen, can be its source. A new leader or team can make strays decide to be a "we." A firm determination to initiate a participatory form of working environment can turn a company away from divisive economism and reroute its aspiration toward solidarity. A shared tragedy can force people out of self-regard and into a sense of relief, purpose, and appreciation of "those of us who are left." The common note in each of these is the evocation of affections or disaffections. We are moved to assent by values but we are moved to action by affections.

Less dramatic proof of solidarity's affective root can be seen in the effect of top management's behavior on the behavior of the corporation. In the corporate world, there is much more imitative behavior than anyone is willing to admit. The power over the whole organization of the CEO's management style or ethical concerns (or for that matter, mismanagement or a lack of ethics) has been noted again and again in management literature. In most corporations, aspiration for or despair about solidarity will depend on the top manager. He or she continually evokes affective response, whether this is recognized or not.

As far as I can determine, Pope John Paul II has been the first to give solidarity the status of a virtue. In fact, he lifts it to a par with charity, the distinguishing virtue Jesus expected in his followers (John 13:35).[31] To be a virtue it must be exercised. The effect of the exercise of the virtue of solidarity is that bonds are forged and the "structures of sin" unravel.[32] Structures of sin proliferate where the desire for profit and the thirst for power" are the operative influences in a given organization.[33] Where this virtue is exercised, workers learn to work by losing themselves for the sake of others. They cease to relate to others in terms of maximizing their own advantage.[34]

The moral status of solidarity requires a recognition of the factual interdependence between persons, groups of persons, and nations. This recognition "is not a feeling of vague compassion or shallow distress" at the misfortune of others.[35] Pope John Paul defines this virtue as "a firm and persevering determination to commit oneself to the common good; that is to say, to the good of all and of each individual because we are all really responsible for all."[36] Solidarity as a virtue begins with the recognition of our interdependence with one another. If acted upon, this recognition will have as its fruit a strengthening of that interdependence.

Both the notion of solidarity, which is at the core of Pope John Paul II's encyclical 1987 *On Social Concerns,* and the notion of econo-mism, found in his 1981 encyclical *On Human Work,* take on new strength when seen in one another's light. While the pope's perspective in the former is worldwide, in the latter it's work-wide. Still, there is much to be gained by applying solidarity to the work scene. Solidarity can dismantle the structures of sin in the work environment. Structures of sin instrumentalize people and transform workers into takers rather than givers to one another and to those served by their work. A virtue that grows strong becomes a habit. When this virtue grows strong among many co-workers, work can be good. Not as good as it was in the Garden, of course, but better than it ordinarily is east of Eden.

# 6

# What Work Lasts?

There is no point in trying to develop a spirituality of work if the work we do has the life span of a sand castle at the ocean's edge. If our daily work is part of what is passing away, a here-today-gone-tomorrow kind of activity, then it's hard to take it very seriously. But isn't this the general attitude in our society about daily work, that it is temporal, necessary, secular, and if you enjoy it, that's the best you can expect from it?

This superficial view of work is not without warrant, even religious warrant. There are many scriptural passages that would seem to confirm this attitude about daily work. For example, "all toil and skillful work is the rivalry of one man for another. This is also vanity and a chase after wind" (Eccles. 4:4). What was said to Adam in the Garden after the Fall is even more discouraging:

> Cursed be the ground because of you! In toil shall you eat its yield all the days of your life. Thorns and thistles shall it bring forth to you as you eat of the plants of the field. By the sweat of your face shall you get bread to eat, until you return to the ground from which you were taken; for you are dirt, and to dirt you shall return." (Gen. 3:17–19)

From this and other texts, work has appeared to be a curse, a necessary exigency, certainly not ennobling nor something of any lasting value.

But this work-is-a-curse view is superficial by comparison to the deeper biblical vision of created reality, our work in it and our use of it, and its future. This deeper vision has two myths that are foundational to it. One of these we have already examined in chapter 2. The myth of our beginnings contained in Genesis is *protological*, meaning "of the first things." The second myth, which we will now examine is *eschatological,* meaning "of the last things," "the end times." Both of these myths are necessary to our understanding of the dignity, stature, and value of human work. If the work we do is somehow of lasting value, it is more noteworthy than if it is over and forgotten upon completion. It is easy enough to see this with famous works, such as the Sistine Chapel or the Declaration of Independence. These have outlasted those whose labors brought them into time. But eschatology is concerned with after time, beyond time. We are interested in the question of what will last of our work beyond time.

If some part of what we work at in time were to become part of the new heaven and the new earth, this would certainly add a new dimension to our work. The question, however, is, Does it? As we saw in our discussion of Genesis, the stature of our work was greatly enhanced when we accepted the protological vision of the goodness of what God has made and God's commission to us to have dominion over it. But the stature of our work would increase even more if we were to assign eschatological value to it.

## Eschatology

First, we will review briefly what we know about eschatology. The kind of eschatology most of us have known has focused on the afterlife of the individual: the possibilities after death were heaven, hell, or purgatory. The world view that conveyed this understanding had several dichotomies to reinforce it, such as the natural versus the supernatural, the soul versus the body, and time versus eternity. Eternity started after time stopped.

In recent years the limitations of this eschatological world view have become apparent. It relies more on metaphysical systems and apocalyptic images than had been suspected. The church is at present in the process of separating these from its doctrine of the last things and is updating its eschatology.[1] I will discuss some of these developments here.

Every renewal of a mystery of faith has been accomplished by a deeper reading of Scripture. We have come to see that most Old Testament eschatology is not concerned with the future and destiny of individuals but with the future and destiny of the people of God and of all peoples. What God inspired in Israel was the expectation of a new terrestrial reality, not something like a next world. Israel looked forward to a future fullness that was social, material, bodily, earthly, and fully human. The people of Israel envisioned a future of a new heaven and a new earth, not all heaven and no earth. Their expectations were usually spelled out in symbolic terms, such as the coming reign of God, a future order that the Messiah would establish, or a reign of eternal peace that a future David would deliver.

Allusions to a future without oppressive toil are not infrequent, for example:

> A people who walked in darkness has seen a great light. . . . For the yoke that burdened them, and the pole on their shoulder, and the rod of their taskmaster you have smashed. . . . For a child is born to us, a son is given us; upon his shoulder dominion rests. (Isa. 9:1–5)

A secondary vein of eschatology developed late in the Old Testament. From what scholars have learned about apocalyptic literature in this century, chiefly by greater knowledge of the social context of its development, they have been able to distinguish it from the rest of Old Testament eschatology. Apocalyptic and the social conditions which spawned it are germane to our theme.[2] A deep despair about the value of work and the effort at building a nation or a civilization characterized this period. This came about because of wanton, irreversible destructiveness by those who were seen as barbarians. All of the efforts of Israel to build itself up as a people had been for naught. So of what value was human labor? Apocalyptic literature, therefore, devised a rescue executed by God who would bring his people away from everything that had been done by them or to them. They would be brought into a new form of existence that canceled out the old efforts to build "the city of man." Since history ended up in chaos, this rescuing God would intervene after it self-destructed.

Christology is the field of study that first yielded fruit in this differentiation between apocalyptic and eschatology. Jesus was seen to have been an eschatological prophet because the coming of God's reign was at the core of his message. He also inaugurated this reign:

"The Kingdom of God is in your midst" (Luke 17:21). Christ's coming radically transformed how we view time. In him eternity had entered into time. Those who clung to him already had eternity in their grasp: "You have died and your life lies hidden with Christ in God" (Col. 3:3) With his coming into the world, a new kind of history is begun, an eschatological history.

By living a life of faith in him and attaching their hopes to him and acting out of love of him, Christians brought a new stature to their actions and, therefore, to their work. The stature of their work and actions was eschatological because work was done through, with, and in him who was and is as eternal as the Father who sent him. That meant that in him his followers participated in this same eternity.

Paul the Apostle reflected early and deeply on this whole matter of what Christ did to time. He believed that Christians must stop assessing themselves "in terms of mere human judgment" since "if anyone is in Christ, he is a New Creation. The old order has passed away; now all is new" (2 Cor. 5:16–17). All of life in this new creation, including work, must be included in this reassessment. A Christian's work, therefore, has the new creation as the base from which it is done, and Christ is part of it. He was not to be a solitary instance but, by God's design, he was "the first born among many" (Rom. 8:29). To be in Christ, therefore, invites much reflection about all that is done in Christ. Our work done through this new way of being can never be assessed in former ways nor with former categories of judgment.

The event that says most to us about our future and its conditions is Jesus' resurrection. We posit our hopes in him with this mystery as the event that most reveals to us what is in store for us. The resurrection is the raising of the whole person of Jesus, body and spirit, into union with God. It is his bodily resurrection, in particular, that provokes a reflection about the future of our works.

It was not only Jesus' body that rose, so also did the body of his works. They lived after him. They have an eternity to them; they are both in history and beyond it. The continuance of his social, ecclesial body is evidence that the body of his works has an eternity in time.

Is there any comparison between his works and ours? Yes and no. No, because of the unique mission he had. Yes, because the life he has given us to live is his own, and the new creation into which this life brings us is as eternal as the Lord of this new creation. And yes, because with this life as his gift to us, he promised "greater works [than mine] will you do" (John 14:12). If he did not think of our works as having less dignity than his—in fact, he claimed they were greater—why do we?

After the resurrection he shows his body to his followers, the hands and feet that had been pierced by the nails and the side that had been run through with the spear. These were the limbs and the body that had labored at the things his Father wanted for the sake of an eternal harvest. He produced fruit that lasted. The Father promised that nothing would be lost of what the Son would do and gain by way of harvest. The resurrection is the symbol that teaches us what will last, what will rise on the Last Day, or, more exactly, what to hope will last: the whole us, body and spirit, and what somehow expresses us, namely, what we have done with what God has given us.

The work the Son was sent to do, the hour for which all the previous hours were anticipatory, was the work of redeeming us. Not only did it endure, but it became the basis of our whole salvation. We are saved even now because even now this work *is;* it continues to be, and it continues to effect our redemption. The glorified hands and side and feet say this to one who has eyes to see. If this work in which and through which we have our future were to pass away, then the new heaven and the new earth that are contingent on it are a mental projection of very foolish folks.

### New Testament Evidence

We will consider some New Testament texts in order to break the spell of pessimism about the world and our actions in it that apocalyptic eschatology or simple melancholy prompts. Paul's letter to the Romans notes:

the whole created world eagerly awaits the revelation of the sons of God. Creation was made subject to futility . . . yet [it is] not without hope, because the world itself will be freed from its slavery to

corruption and share in the glorious freedom of the children of God.
(Rom. 8:19–21)

The picture of the future found here is one in which there is a
continuum between the present, when we and all of creation are
"groaning," and the end times in which we will somehow be included and the reason for groaning will have ceased. Creation's
hopes will not be mocked by annihilation any more than ours will
be. But if the first creation has reason to hope, how much more
should there be hope for a second creation, which is the result of
humans shaping the first creation by their labors. It, too, will
somehow be part of this eschatological scenario. We are not given a
clear understanding of how the present will be factored into the
future, only an indication that it will be. But this is all we need; it is
the only encouragement we need to believe our work has a value
beyond the here and now.

Matthew's Gospel hints at still another dimension of New Testament eschatology. Jesus described the reign of God as being "like
yeast which a woman took and kneaded into three measures of flour.
Eventually the whole mass of dough began to rise" (Matt. 13:33).
The future reign is already here but it is here the way yeast is,
hidden in the massive lump of the world. What are we to do? We are
to knead eternity into the world until it becomes inextricable from it
and both share the same destiny. The yeast is not to enjoy its own
eternity but must lose itself in the dough of time through the
kneading hands of those who carry the reign of God within them.
They do this by their work, by what they work at, as they bring the
yeast into every portion of the dough.

Those to whom the yeast of the reign of God has been given are an
essential component in the process whereby the world is freed from
its "slavery to corruption" (Rom. 8:21), that is, from the mortality
and corruptibility that is endemic to material reality. Those to whom
the yeast has been given did not produce the yeast. Nor did they
earn it. Nor can they make the dough rise. All of this is beyond their
powers. What they can and must do, however, is to take the gift that
has been freely given them by God and knead it into the structures
of time.

Each kneader has a role to play in bringing about the end result, which is the fully risen loaf. Just as the leaven cannot be extricated from the kneaded dough, so also it is not for individuals to seek to extricate themselves from the destiny of the whole, the fate of this world. The yeast was given to be lost in the whole, not to be raised or glorified in isolation. The salvation of wholes, the destiny of the whole, has more scriptural warrant than the salvation of souls. To live and die in the Lord is no small thing when this living and dying has involved working with the yeast that is the life of eternity conferred in time.

Which of our works last? All our works, since we are in the new creation? Just some of our works? The answer is not clear. Some texts in the New Testament emphasize the importance of the works that give expression to the saving faith. For example, in the Book of Revelation a voice from heaven exclaims, "Write this down: Happy now are the dead who die in the Lord!" (Rev. 14:13). The Spirit added, "Yes, they shall find rest from their labors, for their good works accompany them."

Which of our works are good works? A Pauline text contains intriguing comment on this question. In the First Letter to the Corinthians, Paul takes one of the favorite symbols of apocalyptic, the Day of the Lord, together with some very nonapocalyptic ideas to alleviate the pessimism about the value of human efforts. He warns those who are to come after him to be sure that they build on what he has started:

> On this foundation, different people may build in gold, silver, jewels, wood, hay, or straw but each man's handiwork will be shown for what it is. The Day which dawns with fire will make it clear and the fire itself will test the quality of each person's work. The one whose work stands up to it will be given his wages; the one whose work is burnt down will suffer the loss of it." (1 Cor. 3:12–15)

The works that will last, that will survive the fire breaking in upon us on the Day of the Lord, are those that have built on and added to the building that is the Lord's. The works that do not endure are those which were not in alignment with the foundation of the building God was building through his servants. In other words, "Unless the Lord builds the house, they labor in vain who build it" (Ps. 127:1).

Paul sees some human works persisting, enduring after the Day of Judgment. These seem to be those linked to the upbuilding of the body of Christ. But as his vision of the future includes all of creation (as we saw from the text in Romans 8), it is doubtful that the foundation that will last is ecclesial in the narrow sense of the term. Interestingly, Paul even envisions a situation in which a person's works do not survive the refiner's fire but the person does: "The one whose work is burnt down will suffer the loss of it, though he himself will be saved" (1 Cor. 3:14).

A final text, from the same letter, comments further on what it is that makes some works last and others vanish along with all that is passing away. In the first three verses of First Corinthians 13, a number of the most esteemed works in the Christian repertoire of good works are cited; these include speaking with angelic tongues, prophesying, and giving everything one has to feed the poor. In verse 8, however, these works are described as ceasing to be, or passing away, because the one who had done them did not have love. Even more explicitly, Paul says that works done in love "never fail" (1 Cor. 13:8).

A key principle for understanding Paul's eschatology and the specific question of works that last is put forward at the end of this passage. Paul indicates the norm by which he makes his discernment about what will last and what will fail to last. "There are in the end three things that last: faith, hope, and love, and the greatest of these is love" (1 Cor. 13:13). It seems that it is not the acts of faith, hope, and love in themselves that last, but rather works done in faith, hope, and love: it is not the pure intention alone, nor is it faith, hope, and love residing unexercised as three infused theological virtues in a person that last. What lasts is the action taken on these virtues, the praxis that flows from the intention, the works the virtues shape. These last!

What we do not know and will not know in time is what these works done in faith, hope, and love truly look like. This information is no more procurable than knowledge of what our glorified bodies will look like. Thirty years of work at a factory, the arduous and uncertain work of raising one's kids, years of research on a work that never came together, teaching in a school that was phased out—what will any of these works look like, what of them will last, when the new heavens and the new earth come to be? The fact is, we don't know. Nor do we need to. The need is not for sight, wonderful as that would be, but for hope. We hope for immortality, for our bodies to be glorified, and for what we have done to have lasting value. These hopes make the present better, more optimistic, and more tolerable when things are difficult. We also know from experience how thin the present can become when there is no hope for a better future, even if we do not know its shape or the time of its coming.

There is a further dimension to this future and the question of what will last. We have concentrated on the works we do and their eschatological efficacy. There is another whole range of experiences that have perhaps an even greater efficacy than the work we have done. These are the things that happen to us—"acts of God," as the lawyers describe inexplicable catastrophes—injustices done to us, things suffered at the hands of others, incapacities we were born with, competencies that were always beyond our abilities. How do they factor into this eschatological future?

What we suffer and what is done unto us—all of the kinds of events or experiences enumerated above about which we had no choice other than to endure them—these must be borne with the same faith, hope, and love as the works we do. It is the faith with which they are handled, the hope that is retained while they do their unwanted thing, and the love with which we accept them that give these experiences lasting value.

This seems to be the import of some of the Beatitudes. While some Beatitudes describe courses of action (for example, peacemaking), most describe the eternal value of actions taken against us:

> Blest are those persecuted for holiness' sake; the reign of God is theirs. Blest are you when they insult you and persecute you and utter every kind of slander against you because of me. Be glad and rejoice, for your reward is great in heaven." (Matt. 5:10–12)

The mention of reward in this last Beatitude should be noted. It seems to me that this reward paradigm for interpreting our future with God has been a major reason why Christianity has ignored the eschatological value of what we do in time. As long as the only question that is asked about our work is the extrinsic one of reward, the intrinsic one we are asking here is not posed. The closest one comes to it is whether it will make any difference to anyone after I am gone that I have done this or that.

Concern with the matter of reward seems less than mature and highly individualistic. It is focused on the moral value of the work rather than its objectively ontological, eschatological value.[3]

Certainly the reward paradigm is in the New Testament. A partial explanation for this is the fact that the first two generations of Christians entertained fervid expectations of the imminent second coming of Jesus, in light of which their own earthly works seemed less important. The composition of the four Gospels was well underway before these expectations began to weaken. Reward as a paradigm for the relationship between our present actions and our future life in God lost some of its attraction as Christ's coming was delayed. The Gospels of Luke and John especially reflect the change.

For these reasons another paradigm joined or even overtook the reward paradigm. It might be called the recomposition paradigm. Heaven and earth will be recomposed, will be made new. The God who created with no materials will now recompose the first creation with the materials from the second creation developed over time and supplied by the work of human hands. Our work has eschatological meaning if it is part of this recomposition.

Today, most Christians seem to be comfortable with rewarding virtue with eternal life and vice with eternal death. Sometimes one reward is given to those who have done "good works," like feeding the hungry and clothing the naked and contributing to the support of the pastor; those who have failed to do these good works may get the other reward. Where does this leave just plain old daily work? Does it have intrinsic theological worth? Unfortunately, this paradigm leaves it stuck in the middle of nowhere, unless we can come to more depth about its value.

## Conciliar and Theological Contributions

Greater depth and insight into our faith ordinarily come from the teaching church and the theological community. But the spirituality of work has only begun to be addressed in these circles, and what has been elaborated to date is far from satisfying or complete. This is where the reader comes in and why the reflection of workers is encouraged here.

A good beginning for a renewal of eschatology was made by Vatican II. The council insisted on the inseparability of "the temporal and the spiritual orders," seeing them as "so connected in the one plan of God that He Himself intends in Christ to appropriate the whole universe into a new creation, initially here on earth, fully on the last day."[4] The council became more specific when it spoke about cultures. Whatever is beautiful, true and good in human cultures will be cleansed, perfected, and transfigured, and become part of the new creation. Our work in time is part of "the body of a new human family, a body which even now is able to give some kind of foreshadowing of the new age."[5] If by our labors we have

> nurtured on earth the values of human dignity, brotherhood, and freedom, and indeed all the good fruits of our nature and enterprise, we will find them again, but freed of stain, burnished and trans-figured. This will be so when Christ hands over to the Father a kingdom eternal and universal.[6]

In twentieth-century theology, eschatology has come into its own. Many theologians subscribe to Jürgen Moltmann's proposition that "the eschatological is not one element of Christianity, but it is the medium of Christian faith."[7] Through this medium we read ourselves, God, time, our activity in the world, and the world itself.

Johannes Metz was one of the notable contributors to this trend to reinstate eschatology. He based his political theology in eschatology, specifically in the hopes of those who through their actions and witness anticipate the coming Kingdom of God. Those who hope do justice to the fullness all await if they act militantly, creatively, and productively. They do not do it justice if they await the New Jerusalem passively. As Metz puts it,

> We are workers building this future and not just interpreters of this future. The power of God's promises for the future moves us to form this world into the eschatological city of God.[8]

Although his theology doesn't address the meaning of work as such, Metz's general observations about human efforts are germane to the issue. Our actions must be posited in hope. They must bring our hopes for the Kingdom of God to the fore. Our hopes must be in God, but not in such a way that we fail to take action. This kingdom will not come without our efforts, even though it is not our efforts that will bring it about.

> The orthodoxy of a Christian's faith must constantly make itself true in the orthopraxy of his actions oriented towards the final future, because the promised truth is a truth which must be made.[9]

Truth must be done to be truth (John 3:21). True thinking is orthodoxy; orthopraxy is true doing, or truth done.

For Christians, Metz observes, hope is very different from the "militant optimism" of many who are out to transform the world. These optimists posit their hopes in the works done by themselves and others. Christians posit their hopes in the God from whom their hope comes and in whom their hope remains lodged. Christianity does not posit its hopes in a vision of the future. "Hope is not hope if its object is seen" (Rom. 8:24). Our hope doesn't grow in proportion to the specificity of our vision of the future, as is the case with many ideologies.

> What distinguishes the Christian and the other, secular ideologies of the future from one another is not that Christians know more, but that they know less about the sought-after future of humanity and that they face up to this poverty of knowledge.[10]

Christians are like so many little Abrahams, who, having heard the call "went forth not knowing where he was going" (Heb. 11:8).

It took a paleontologist, not a professional theologian, to make twentieth-century eschatology more tangible. Pierre Teilhard de Chardin (1881–1955) constructed a beautiful religious vision of work from a combination of sources: his interior spiritual life, his professional scientific life, and his personal and ecclesial experiences. The result is a mélange of intuitions that mix evolution and eschatology in an original way. Its originality should stimulate our own inchoate vision at this point in our study.

Teilhard saw all human endeavors as driven by hope:

No man would lift his little finger to attempt the smallest task unless he were spurred on by a more or less obscure conviction that in some infinitesimally tiny way he is contributing, at least indirectly, to the building up of something permanent—in other words, to your own work, Lord.[11]

He saw the hope in human actions complemented by the strivings of the infrahuman universe of things, both moving according to their respective inner endowments, heading somewhere, going somewhere. Unbeknownst to them, they were going in the same direction and acting toward a common end, which he called Omega point.

At point Alpha in the evolutionary process God began to create out of a "physical nothingness." Evolutionary energies also began then and moved in the direction of ever greater complexity, order, consciousness, and freedom. In the course of this long process, spirit will eventually "dethrone" matter. It will also become increasingly "personal," the person being none other than Christ. Point Omega, it turns out, is him.[12]

Human creation, and material creation with it, was moving forward. They were also moving upward at the same time, attracted consciously or unconsciously toward something that transcended them. Teilhard loved the earth in all its parts: even in an inert rock he saw these dual drives of forward and upward, the striving and its end point. The more he found out about bones, the more he found God in them. All matter, he concluded, was charged with the energy of God the Creator and the Incarnate Word. Our world, therefore, is a divine, not a profane, milieu.

One of the actions Teilhard himself performed communicates some of these sentiments. On one of his many scientific expeditions he found himself alone in the desert without the elements he needed to offer the Eucharist, which, at the time, he felt a great need to offer. Hyperconscious of the presence of Christ in the physical world that surrounded him, he decided he would make the whole earth serve as the altar. Instead of bread and wine he offered his own labors and sufferings as well as those of all people throughout the world.[13] He felt his offering was accepted and blessed by God. He had been in the practice of offering his own and others works and their suffering to God so that these might be consecrated. He never tired in his aspirations to make the divine milieu more an object of consciousness than it presently is.

One of the most attractive aspects of Teilhard's vision is his intuition about the role of love in the attainment of the end time toward which all things are a vector. Love is what makes parts into a whole. He asks,

> To what power is it reserved to burst asunder the envelopes in which our individual microcosms tend jealousy to isolate themselves and to vegetate? To what force is it given to merge and exalt our partial rays into the principal radiance of Christ?[14]

Love, Teilhard answered! Love was, for him, the source and consequence of every spiritual relationship. Even more revealing is his wholistic vision of the Omega point, when the dough is fully risen with the yeast of love: "The only subject ultimately capable of spiritual transfiguration is the totality of mankind forming together a single body and a single soul in charity."[15]

Christianity, for Teilhard, entered into the evolutionary process at a predesigned moment as a phylum of love. "Christianity is nothing more nor less than a phylum of love within nature."[16] One synonym he used for the Omega point was "theossphere of love."[17] Love has the happy facility of uniting what it touches and, at the same time, enabling that which is becoming unified to also become more differentiated, more itself, attaining its uniqueness.

He became increasingly interested in the connection between the energy of love and the world's coming to maturity. The more people were "de-centered," as he put it, from themselves and centered on the other, ultimately on the cosmic Christ, the more whole they become. He coined the word *amorization* to describe the process in persons and communities in which their actions move from occasional gestures of love to continual loving. The greater our power to love, the greater is Christ's hold over the universe.[18]

He found that God could be found in every aspect of one's work.

> God presents himself to us as attainable through our very work . . .
> God . . . awaits us in every instant in our action, in the work of the
> moment. There is a sense in which he is at the tip of my pen, my

spade, my brush, my needle—of my heart and of my thought. By pressing the stroke, the line or the stitch on which I am engaged, to its ultimate natural finish, I shall lay hold of the last end toward which my innermost will tends.[19]

He insisted on the need to have one's faith in Christ and one's love of him come to bear explicitly on what one did in the world. No less important was the intention of the worker. Intention is the "golden key" that opens the soul to the experience of the immanent presence of God in the world.[20] Or, to change metaphors, he believed that "the divinization of our endeavors by the value of the intention put into them, pours a priceless soul into all our actions."[21]

Teilhard asks the same searching question we asked at the outset of this chapter:

It is certainly a very great thing to be able to think that, if we love God, something of our inner activity will never be lost. But will not the work itself of our mind, of our hearts, and of our hands—that is to say, our achievements, what we bring into being, our opus—will not this, too, in some sense be eternalized and saved?[22]

He is sure it will be eternalized, since "if I believed that these things were to perish for ever, should I have even given them life?"[23]

The style and attitude we bring to our work is to be patterned after Christ's own style and attitude. The word that went forth from God's mouth gave itself wholly to earth in the Incarnation. The word did not return to God "void," but filled with the love and service of all to whom he had ministered. One cannot be faithful to God, Teilhard was convinced, unless one is faithful to the earth, as Jesus was. For him this involved his archaeological digs and his research into bones and earth. The rest of us may not experience and appreciate earth as directly as a paleontologist does, but the point holds, nonetheless, that we come to union with God first by descent into "matter" and only then by ascent into communion with God, as did the Son of God.[24] This is why Teilhard encouraged Christians to fan into a burning passion their love of earth and world.

The theological argument he advanced for this "immersion" in earth, and the value of human endeavor it implies, came from his understanding of the Incarnation. This mystery was, among other things, a physical event:

> By his Incarnation he inserted himself not just into humanity but into the universe which supports humanity . . . [as] a directing principle, a Center toward which everything converges in harmony and love.[25]

Therefore, the more one plumbs the earth, the more one should be able to find God since this is where God has permeated through Christ and his Incarnation.

The twin mysteries of creation and Incarnation give work its intrinsic value. Our work on earth, Teilhard would say, is completing Christ—or, through the work we do, Christ is completing himself.[26] Who is this cosmic Christ? Christ is somehow at the physical center of the world. "Between the Word on the one hand and Jesus the Man on the other, a sort of Christic third nature comes into being. . . ."[27] He is not simply "a cosmic element" in the universe. He is, rather, the "ultimate psychic Center for the gathering together of the Universe."[28]

There is one last part of Teilhard's vision of Christ, with its fascinating nexus between the spiritual and the physical world, that should be touched on, namely, the Eucharist. "It is first by the Incarnation and next by the Eucharist that Christ organizes us for himself and imposes himself upon us."[29] In fact, for Teilhard, the whole process of evolution is itself a kind of Mass that has been going on for centuries. In this process, all the elements of the universe are slowly being consecrated into this one cosmic Christ, this third nature that came into being after the resurrection:

> As our humanity assimilates the material world and as the Host assimilates our humanity, the eucharistic transformation goes beyond and completes the transubstantiation of the bread on the altar. Step by step it irresistably invades the universe.[30]

He was not satisfied to let the Eucharist stay a private, nor even a Catholic, rite. It had "a cosmic function" and "planetary dimensions."[31] In his "Mass on the World" he asks God to take the work and travail of the world and transfigure it, "remold it, rectify it, recast it."[32]

Do you now, O Lord, speaking through my lips, pronounce over this earthly travail your twofold efficacious word . . . over every living thing which is to spring up, to grow, to flower, to ripen during this day say again the words: This is my Body. And over every death-force which waits in readiness to corrode, to wither, to cut down, speak again your commanding words which express the supreme mystery of faith: This is my Blood.[33]

And if they are so consecrated, guess how long they last!

# 7

# The Meaning God Sees

The meaning we see in our work is only one part of its meaning. The meaning others see in our work is another. In this chapter, we will ask ourselves what meaning God sees in our work. It would be wonderful to know the answer since success at what we do comes less frequently than we would like and our efforts often seem insignificant. When we ask of God so blunt a question, God answers us but not as directly as we would like. The answer is somehow already contained in the data of revelation which, as we believe, comes from a revealing God. If we wish to know God's mind about work, we can find out much by looking at what the Scriptures say. But even after we have done our best to discern the mind of God about the meaning of our work through the Word of God, we will be left with more that is unknown than known.

In the final analysis God alone knows the meaning of our work. We surrender it to God. How? With a process that is simple, traditional, and profound, but seldom made explicit. (I used this process in my last book, *The Holy Use of Money*.) It is elaborated in a book on Christology titled *Christ Proclaimed*, by Franz Jozef Van Beeck.[1] Van Beeck's thesis is that a healthy Christology develops when we take our this-worldly concerns to the mystery of Christ and rename them in terms of him and him in terms of them. When applied to our financial resources we found that Christ as our wealth made both existential and theological sense. The same process can be applied to this question of work.

There are three steps in the process of surrender and transformation. The first of these is inclusion. Acts of inclusion of my work and work done with co-workers in the mystery of God do not require much explanation. Faith supplies the power that is needed to make such acts. They indicate one's refusal to allow the "secular" activity of work to remain in its own separate, self-contained sphere.

Work, like money, is frequently handled as though it and we were under the seeming sovereignty of the economy. The act of inclusion brings it under a different sovereignty. What had been exclusively my concern, my work, or my business undergoes a change of venue. My work is now also the concern of the One to whom it has been surrendered. Acts of inclusion are done at different levels, of course; some are superficial formalities and others are acts of real committal. The inclusion of our work in God means that it is no longer solely our responsibility. The result should be a shouldering of our work responsibility in a way that is consciously accompanied. Work can now be an exercise in coresponsibility.

There are a number of passages in Scriptures that comment on this action of inclusion of what we and others do in our workplace in the mystery of God. Paul for example, exhorts the Romans to "offer your bodies as a living sacrifice, holy and acceptable to God, your spiritual worship" (Rom. 12:1). *Bodies* here has the specific meaning of actions done with bodies, what touches us and what we touch, shape, use, develop, produce, buy, sell, and so forth. These actions are part of what is to be offered, surrendered, or included in our act of worship. Worship indicates, among other things, that the worshiper deems the One worshiped to be of preeminent worth compared to the things and actions offered. This worship is spiritual because it is worship from the heart, from the spirit, done in the Spirit. It is a living sacrifice because it is done in an ongoing manner. Since our "bodies" are continually doing things, we always have new work to offer. The sacrifice is "holy and acceptable to God" because of its intention and the Spirit that empowers the act.

The next verse indicates the great benefit of acts of inclusion for the person performing them. "Do not conform yourselves to this age but be transformed by the renewal of your mind, so that you may judge what is God's will, what is good, pleasing and perfect" (Rom. 12:2). The one changed by the act of inclusion is not the One to whom the offering is made, but the offerer. The offering is removed from "this age," which Paul described as "passing away," and located in the new age, insofar as the intentionality of the offerer can effect that relocation. Having included one's work in God, it is less likely that one will be conformed to this age. Furthermore, the removal of our work from this age makes possible a "renewal of our mind" about the work, since work can no longer exercise so imperious a hold over us. Finally, Paul indicates that the fruit of inclusion is discernment: "that you may judge what is God's will, what is good, pleasing and perfect." The distance one gains by inclusion sharpens one's ability to judge one's work, its worth, its deficiency, and the manner and spirit in which it should be done. By this distancing one is more able to see it from God's side, or in terms of God's will about it. Consequently, "good, pleasing, even perfect" work becomes more likely.

Acts of inclusion can trigger or reinforce whole new ways of thinking, acting, and living in those who develop them as a habit. Inclusion is a new way of thinking and acting that might be described as an anthropology of entrustment. Inclusion is entrustment, if it is anything. Growth in trust and a strengthening of the bonds of trust between the offerer and God is the main fruit of the habit of inclusion.

But acts of inclusion are not merely for those performing them. They have ministerial efficacy. They are for others. They strengthen the ministerial capacities of the includer, who gains a clearer and deeper perspective in the framework of their truth. By renewing our minds and heightening our capacity to judge our work situations, God can reach out, through and beyond the includer, to shape that which "his hands have made" and the systems within which people live out their lives.

The act of inclusion is an act of participation in the priesthood of Christ. Baptized Christians are empowered to entrust to God all those areas of concern in which they and their co-workers share responsibilities. The individual worker is a part of a larger, more complex branch that draws its life force from the Vine. The portion of the branch that is endowed with the priestly character of Christ offers the whole branch to him who wishes to "draw all" to himself: "And when I am lifted up from the earth I will draw everyone to myself" (John 12:32). The includer is instrumental in Christ's sublational and redemptive intentionality. Having been perfected, our High Priest became "the source of eternal salvation" for all (Heb. 5:9). The people of God who participate in the priesthood of Christ offer to the Father the fruits both of their own labor and that of those who don't know the value of doing this. By doing so, they "consecrate the world itself to God."[2] They do so "through him and with him and in him in the unity of the Holy Spirit" so that "all glory and honor might be the Father's," in the words of the prayer at the end of the Canon of the Mass.

Jesus, who is "the forerunner of our faith" (Heb. 6:20), was in the habit of inclusion, as every portion of the Gospels will attest. Possibly the best illustration of this part of his character is his response to the tempter in the desert (Matt. 4:1–11). He had been entrusted with everything by the Father: "The Father loves the Son and has entrusted everything to his hands" (John 3:35). The response of the Son to the Father was to entrust himself and all that he had and did to the Father. Therefore, "Away with you Satan! Scripture has it: You shall do homage to the Lord your God; Him alone shall you adore!" (Matt. 4:10).

The second act needed in this process of surrendering to God the meaning of our work is that of obedience. It is not enough simply to include our work. We must obey God about the work we have included. Both the work done and the work still to be done are matters for obedience. Before it was included it was my work alone. Once it is included, my work becomes my way of loving God and God's way of loving me. The Old Testament expressed this insight: Israel was commanded by Yahweh to "Love the Lord, your God, with all your heart, and with all your soul, and with all your strength" (Deut. 6:5). To love God "with all our strength" means "with all that we have going for us" by way of status, recognition, accomplishments, skills, and financial and material resources.[3] These strengths are what is included. Hence, their subsequent use is the subject matter for obedience and they assume instrumental value for growing in the love and service of God.

As we have discussed in chapter 2, our work is to obey the command to take dominion over the infrahuman world in collaboration with all other creatures who were made in the image and likeness of their Creator. Our obedience, therefore, has this command as its content. The specific contents differ from person to person and generation to generation.

The obedience of Christians means, then, loving God with our strengths. It would also mean learning about and, insofar as possible, becoming competent in the things relating to one's work and the workplace. The Lord means to be Lord of all things in heaven and earth. One of the ways he intends to do this is through the growing competence of those who count him as their Lord. Learning is a form of obedience that is pleasing to God since it endows the learner with more knowledge of what God has made or more competence to judge the matters they handle or more skills to serve others. Refusal to learn is a form of disobedience to the reality through which God speaks to us and has us serve others. To develop skills is to practice a form of obedience. It is also a way of obeying the commission given all of us to assume dominion over creation.

Another aspect of obedience to the Lord with respect to our work is its moral character. We would hardly be comfortable offering our employer sloppy work, lazy work, defective work, or indifferent work. The same can be said about what we offer The Employer. Implicit in the process begun with inclusion and followed by obedience is the commitment to move beyond comfort, convenience, self-regard, and deficient work to valuable work, valued work, other-regarding work. Obedience to fact and to value are components of our obedience to Christ. The workaday world offers us many ways to obey the Christ to whom we entrust our work. Being self-seeking or greedy in our work, being willfully ignorant about some aspect of it or lazy in developing our competence are some of the ways the step of obedience is not taken.

The third step in this anthropology of entrustment is hope. Christians are empowered to hope in God at baptism. One does not need to be empowered with the theological, infused virtue of hope in order to hope in God, but the virtue emboldens and deepens the natural affinity of the baptized to locate his or her hopes in God. Hope is a virtue, an energy, a power, and a habit only to the extent to which it is exercised.

The theological virtue of hope focuses, empowers, and deepens our hoping. The object of that hope is God. But we hope for more than God even though our hopes are in God. God is the One in whom we ultimately hope. But we have other, proximate objects of hope, some of which are related to our work. Integrating our hope in God with our other hopes is part of what the virtue of hope enables us to do.

We have many work-related hopes. If we are unemployed we may
hope for a job, or we may hope to hold the job we have. We may also
hope for a more meaningful job, for our job to be meaningful to
others or meaningful in God's eyes, to be appreciated on the job and
to be given fair and decent wage, to have justice done to all of our co-
workers, for the insight to see the religious dimension of our work,
for our work to benefit others, or for the work environment to
become one in which all parties are respected, compensated, har-
monious with one another, productive, and happy. Any or all of
these job-related hopes are worthy of us. They are all hopes *for*
something. We can hope for many things. We owe to it ourselves as
followers of Christ to hope for them *in* him. Hoping in him does not
snuff out other hopes; rather, it integrates lesser hopes in him.

Hoping in him also corrects our hopes, even our work-related
hopes. The stronger our hope in God, the fewer and deeper our
other hopes become. Weak hope allows many desires to proliferate.
Saint Thomas Aquinas distinguished *desires*, which are focused on
objects that are proximate and attainable, from *hopes*, which are
focused on objects that are remote and attainable only with considerable difficulty.[4] Saint Paul prayed that the Ephesians would be
granted a vision "of the great hope to which he has called you, and
the wealth of his glorious heritage to be distributed among the
members of the church" (Eph. 1:18). Doesn't that sound wonderful?

Plural hopes, needless hopes, and desire-heavy hopes all seem to
be included in Jesus' use of the symbol Kingdom of God: "Your
heavenly Father knows all that you need. Seek first his kingship over
you, his way of holiness, and all these things will be given you
besides" (Matt. 6:32–33). Jesus did not preach a spiritualization of
human hopes, just a purification and simplification of them. The
pearl merchant learned how to go from little, scattered, faint hopes
to one overpowering one (Matt. 13:45–46). If we sought out God and
God's agenda as the focus of our lives, our hearts would know that all
our lesser hopes and needs will be satisfied, are satisfied, by the
One who makes us such passionate hopers. If we have at all succeeded in finding him for whom "my flesh pines and my soul thirsts"
(Ps. 63:2), we will find ourselves trusting more, needing less, and
becoming impatient with our own niggling anxiety. Any real experience of God functions like a divining rod that enables us to sort out

the hopes that should be given room in our hearts from those that
should be shown the door. Any authentic experience of God inten-
sifies our valid hope but breaks open narrow hopes, skewers false
hopes, and corrects ill-conceived hopes. It encourages the hope to
give and discourages the hope to have. It discourages efforts at
hoping to be important, recognized, autonomous, in control. It fans
any flame that loves, serves, and listens.

Meaning itself isn't a scriptural category. Rather, scriptural categories make meaning when they are appropriated. One of the
themes of Scripture relevant to work's meaning, is that of the glory of
God. It is an ordinary human experience to want to glorify ourselves
by something we are trying to accomplish, but this intentionality
can also be displaced. We can seek to bring honor and glory on
another by something we are trying to achieve. Children, for example, can fiercely desire to bring honor to their parents by winning a
class prize. Athletes can seek to bring honor to their country by
winning a gold medal. Workers can seek to bring honor to God by
their work.

"The fact is that whether you eat or drink—whatever you do—you
should do all for the glory of God" (1 Cor. 10:31). This intentionality
can grow strong. It can become constant. Doing all for the glory of
God can supercede all other intentionalities operating in us. Although it does not cancel other intentionalities that we bring to the
work we do, if it is substantial it will align them and integrate them.
Working for the glory of God will reduce anxiety about being disparaged or overlooked or passed up since seeking my own honor and
glory is sublimated by the desire to honor and glorify God by my
work. When we work for the glory of God, it heightens our consciousness about the significance of the work done in our firm or
factory or business: we become less tolerant of work that is over-
priced or defective, or that degrades those doing it.

As one seeks to glorify God by one's work, one offers a prayer of
praise subliminally throughout the work day. The subliminal praise
of God that comes from intending our work to give glory to God is
like a fragrance holy and pleasing to God. The command to work for
God's glory is as important as the command to have dominion. These
are the most appropriate intentionalities we can bring to work. We
are merely servants of God's dominion and the more clearly we see

this purpose for our lives, and the more we glorify God. "In all of you God is to be glorified through Jesus Christ: to him be glory and dominion throughout the ages. Amen" (1 Pet. 4:11).

The process of inclusion, obedience, and hope brings us into the mystery of Christ, whose glory already fills heaven and earth (Ps. 19:2). The transformation of the world is a process in which the initial glory that permeates the world is compounded by those who invest themselves in it. The mediators God has placed in history are to trace this glory to its source. And when Christ comes again, he will come in glory—a glory that accrues to him over time because includers, obeyers, and hopers insist that it is his.

# 8

# A Spirituality of Work

People work all day long and all week long, in most cases, for all of their lives. People of faith also work all day long, all week long, all of their lives. Two main reasons for working are because we have to or because we want to. The religious reasons for daily work are less clear.

This volume has suggested a series of reflections that working people can use to begin to clarify and shape their own spirituality of work. Every worker already has an implicit or informal spirituality of work. The human spirit of each worker inevitably assigns a meaning and a value to his or her work, including work deemed to have little or no meaning and little or no value. My intention has been to bring what is usually implicit out into the open and to make work an object of reflection. As this process becomes more explicit, people of faith eventually connect their understanding of their work to their understanding of God. By undertaking a sustained, systematic reflection on the religious meaning of our daily work, we are able to develop a spirituality of work in the formal sense of that term.

Such reflection must be based on personal experience to keep it from becoming an ideology. An ideology of work would be a theory fashioned somewhere, somehow, by people ignorant of my experience. If I were to subscribe to their understanding I would have to impose it on my own work situation with the very likely result that it would create an awkwardness for me or for my co-workers.

A spirituality of work has to be created *by* the worker not *for* the worker. This study will seek to provide a method for reflection on such a spirituality. This reflection will have to include both one's own experience and the data that would give it religious objectivity. Such data will be theological. If our reflection ignored personal work experience the result would be a theology of work. A spirituality, on the other hand, is based on our understanding of God, the theological data that surround this understanding, plus our actual or intended response to that data in the course of living and working.

People whose faith is important to them have varying degrees of insight into the religious meaning of their daily work. This study hopes to make these insights more explicit, methodical, critical, and dimensional. For example, some people practise a general form of offering of their work to God. This "morning offering" is as far as many have gotten in connecting their work and their faith. Others are attracted to the notion of serving others as the core of the religious meaning of their work. Both orientations are good starting points, but there is much more to the link between work and faith than these two attitudes. In this volume, we have explored these other orientations and attitudes.

## Is This Trip Really Necessary?

Why should someone want to develop a spirituality of work? I can think of a dozen good reasons.

1. Work is usually assumed to be a this-worldly, secular activity. This assumption deceives many. A spirituality of work supercedes this superficial assessment of work held by so many Americans. It articulates an understanding that is concrete and relevant for the religious meaning of one's daily work.

2. Deepening the religious meaning of one's work makes it possible for one's work to be an occasion for growth in faith, hope, and love—in a word, for union with God. The usual assessments of work seldom see it having that potentiality. Without a spirituality of work, our union with God is put into cold storage until we are in more conducive, that is, religious, circumstances.

3. A better integration of our faith with our work brings many of the strengths of faith to bear on the work situation. Values such as honesty, loyalty, industry, integrity, patience, and charity are but a few of the virtues that religion seeks to cultivate and that the work culture sorely needs.

4. Those who are overinvested in work are in need of something that enables them to put this part of their lives in perspective. Religion can be a major resource for gaining perspective and keeping it.

5. Those who are underinvested in their work need something that will motivate them to apply themselves more diligently to that for which they are salaried. Doing a day's work for a day's pay is a simple matter of justice, something every religious faith has addressed. Faith should function as a corrective for the indolent or bored, to make them more industrious in their work.

6. Religion gives the believer a way to measure all aspects of life. It is a source of norms. Religious reflection on work should help workers take stock not only of how they work but also, perhaps more importantly, of what their work is doing to them.

7. People are subjects surrounded by objects. Subjects make meaning; objects have their meanings given to them by subjects. Workers are surrounded by objects whose meaning should be assigned them by workers. Faith is the major resource available to believer subjects for making meaning and for assigning meaning to their lives, the things that touch their lives, and the work they do.

8. A spirituality of work would help to develop one's sensitivity to the social purposes of work, primarily its purpose in serving the needs of people. Contributive justice is the responsibility of everyone and one's job is the ordinary way one has of contributing to the common good.[1]

9. Spiritual integration and cognitive integration go hand in hand. An integration of faith and work involves a cognitive process, one that seeks to see as a whole the many parts of the worker's life. This is precisely what a spirituality of work attempts to develop.

10. We must see and savor the sacramental character of all created things. To do so requires a recall of the relevant Scriptures, doctrines, and theological reflections that enable us to see work-related things anew, and in a sacramental light.

11. An inability to see the sacral meaning of one's work reduces its meaning to secularity and immanence. "A job is a job is a job," is the only thing you can say about it. This position inevitably forces those who consider themselves religious into a kind of spiritual or intellectual schizophrenia. To leave parts of one's life disconnected diminishes one's spiritual growth and one's productivity as a worker.

12. Alternate views of success and failure are invaluable for freeing oneself from the kinds of bondage people often find in work situations. (I am referring to being riffed or demoted or plateaued or even fired.) Religious faith is able to supply other standards of success or failure. Thus some of the stigma or threat that a single source of self-evaluation provides is more easily managed.

While all of these reasons for developing a spirituality of work are cogent, we could ask whether we were meant to develop such an instrument. Does God want us to be equipped with this? Is it necessary for the full living out of one's faith? The answer should be obvious. If we spend six-sevenths of our time working, should we not have an explicit faith understanding of the meaning of such a large part of our lives?

One of the most explicit passages in the New Testament on the meaning of our work describes it as bearing fruit. The fuller metaphor is that of the vine and the branches. Jesus describes his Father as "the vinegrower" who is busy pruning the branches so that they will "increase their yield" (John 15:1–2). The passage goes on to advise his followers, "Live on in me, as I do in you. No more than a branch can bear fruit of itself apart from the vine, can you bear fruit apart from me" (John 15:4).

It would be hard to find a better image for summing up a spirituality of work. It sums up its purpose and value. Barren branches do not glorify God. There is no comparison between the efficacy of the work done by the branch that is firmly attached to the vine and that done by the branch that is broken off. The purpose of this volume is to stimulate some of the reflection needed to secure the branches to the vine deeply and permanently.

In this volume *work* means "the productive activity people do." Productive activity can be salaried or unsalaried. Raising a family, for example, is certainly work and it is certainly productive. What is said about work in this volume will usually be a comment on salaried work because this is the area that is most infrequently and inadequately related to spirituality. But everything that is said about salaried work applies equally to the many forms of unsalaried work that are so productive of a good society, from the most difficult jobs of making a home and raising a family to voluntary service.

Productive activity stands in sharp contrast to unproductive activity. The latter occurs when our employment either asks nothing of us as persons or is done listlessly and without input from our faculties of imagination, mind, or will. This unproductivity can be due to either the nature of the work or, as is more often the case, the manner in which one chooses to work. In either case, this study will be of little use to such workers since their humanity is so underinvested in their work that our considerations here will be largely irrelevant to their work experience.

## Precedents

Theological reflection on the subject of work is virtually unknown in both formal theology and in pastoral practice. There seem to be four major reasons for this.

The most ancient reason is that the classical world, Plato and Aristotle in particular, did not esteem labor. The human activities they did esteem were politics, the arts, and the intellectual life.[2] Philosophers contended that manual labor, while necessary, made workers virtually indistinguishable from animals. The fact is that most manual labor in their day was done by slaves.

This Greek bias against regular, pedestrian, necessary work deeply affected Western civilization. In particular, it affected the early centuries of Christianity. Christians developed a deep esteem for the activity of contemplation. If the act of contemplation is the most noble act a person can perform and if the beatific vision of God is the zenith of human experience, then everyday pedestrian work suffers by comparison.[3] Work as such was not only despised as something for peasants and slaves but, at the same time, it received virtually no theological attention from the early church fathers.

The manner in which theology has been done since the Middle Ages is a second reason for the virtual nonexistence of a spirituality of work. Theology has always been an exercise in which faith seeks understanding, but it did not develop as a systematic intellectual discipline until the twelfth century. Earlier theology had taken religious experience more into account and drew from religious understandings as these were experienced and articulated through, in, and as a result of personal and liturgical prayer. Personal experi-

ence as we understand it today was not as important for theology
after the twelfth century. These ages were not equipped for the kind
of introspection or consciousness that is necessary for the reflection
on experience we are speaking of here. After the Middle Ages,
Scripture and tradition were seen as a much tidier and objective
source of data than the unrecorded, inchoate, subjective data of
one's own life and experience.

Several twentieth-century developments have begun to change
this abstract way of going about theology. The West has become
much more aware of the biases and limitations of its epistemology.
For one thing, it has begun to be affected by developments within
the third world, especially its penchant for an experience-centered
way of pursuing truth. Instead of a theology formulated by scholars,
applied by pastors, and lived out by still others who have received
their understanding from these leaders, a new way is developing. It
is in part a process of reflection on the relationship between faith
and work, although it also goes by the more sophisticated name of
dialectical reflection, which connects revolutionary praxis and critical theory. (We will examine this at greater length in the next
chapter.)

Another modern influence on Roman Catholic theology has been
the Second Vatican Council and some of the categories it validated. I
have in mind the new clarity the church developed about such
notions as its role in the world, the vocation of the laity, the exten-
sion of the understanding of ministry, and the autonomy of the
secular. All of these have contributed to processes of theological
reflection that are centered on experience. These processes have
expanded the usual way of doing theology beyond what is done by
professionals in much the same way that ministry has been extended
beyond what is done by ordained ministers. As a result, what
Christians do in the world, and the world in which they do it, are
now seen as valid objects of theological reflection. The division of
labor, if we may call it that, among laity, pastors, and theologians is
in a fortuitous disarray. Theology, consequently, is less elitist. It has
developed a new appreciation of experience, in this case, the experience of work "in the world."

A third reason for the absence of a spirituality of work is something of an irony. The popes of the Roman Catholic church have

developed a series of positions in the last hundred years in documents called social encyclicals. Many of these encyclicals are comments on the social conditions of work and workers. The effect of this
papal concentration on both the theological community and the
faithful in general was to leave untouched the equally important
matter of the religious meaning of daily work. Papal attention was
directed to the morality of the social conditions of workers and not to
their personal spirituality. While the personal spirituality of the
worker and the morality of the social conditions of work intersect at
some places, they are quite different. The irony is that the papal
object of attention commandeered so much attention that the other
area of the terrain—namely, the spirituality of the worker—has been
largely neglected.

There were some attempts made by theologians in the late 1950s
and early 1960s to fashion a theology of work. During this period
biblical theologies of all kinds were elaborated. The strength of these
theologies lay in the power of Scripture and in their positive evaluation of work. Their weakness was threefold. First, they were not
experience based, and the use of biblical or theological sources that
are not experience based creates a kind of transcendental or ascetic
ideology. Second, they did not invite workers to do the social
analysis of the workplace that was needed to make a theology of work
responsive to the actual work situation. Finally, as biblical scholars
have come to appreciate, the use of the Bible to do theologies of this
or that misuses Scripture. It tends to conflate biblical themes irrespective of the contexts within which they were developed. As a
result, these efforts at biblical theologies of work were not successful.[4]

A fourth and final reason for the almost total neglect of work as a
subject for theology is the intimate connection between the economy and one's job. There seems to be a variation on the notion of
separation between church and state that functions as a cultural
axiom. To put it crudely, this axiom states: Jobs are part of the
economy, and the economy is its own law, answering to no higher or
other law; therefore jobs are outside, or beyond the pale of, morality, Gospel, or divine providence. It would be a breach of the wall
that maintains the separation of church and state to have one's job
become responsive to another law higher than that of the free
market.

In their 1986 letter "Economic Justice for All," the American Catholic bishops breached that wall by daring to make a moral assessment of the American economy. They refused to subscribe to the dogma that "economic life is an autonomous realm which, for the most part, should be allowed to run on its own, without interference from external influences—like religion."[5] The present volume will be guilty of the same impropriety.

## Characteristics of a Spirituality of Work

Before we proceed further, it would be helpful to specify the characteristics a spirituality of work should have. First of all, as has already been suggested, it would have to be personally composed. It cannot be done for me, it must be done by me. If it were to be done by another for me it would either be wanting in specificity and therefore unusable or it would be too specific and the use of it would impose something alien on the actual situations I find myself in at work.

Such a spirituality also has to be experience based. This necessary characteristic poses a question about how something can be at once both experience based and objective, an issue that we will deal with subsequently. Suffice it to say here that recent developments in theology have begun to fashion methodologies that take experience into account. This is necessary, since experience of itself is neither reflective, critical, nor objective. Nevertheless, to ignore experience is as hazardous to the health of the church and to the field of theology as it is to people.

A further characteristic of such a theology is that it would have to be developed with the help of publically accessible texts. Some of these might include the stated mission and objectives of an employing company, its code of ethics or that of an industry or a profession. Other important texts include the Scriptures and doctrines of the church, and the church's teachings germane to the world of work. Two useful documents for Roman Catholics in this matter of work are Pope John Paul II's "On Human Work" (1981) and the American Catholic bishops' 1986 pastoral letter on the economy that has already been mentioned.

The importance of public documents brings us to a further characteristic of this work spirituality: it must be social. The antithesis of social is *private*, which connotes deprivation and, for that reason, deficiency. A spirituality of work is done from an experience of working, and most work experiences are social. People usually work with other people. While each brings his or her own values and purposes to the situation, a spirituality of work has to have enough objectivity to be communicable to one's colleagues. Even if others show no interest in it, the content of one's spirituality must be sufficiently objective and coherent to be communicable. Arcane, subjective, unintelligible understandings do justice neither to oneself and others nor to the faith itself. While we must admit that our own spirituality is more unknown than known even to ourselves, nonetheless a complete inability to articulate the portion that is known—or an inability to make it understandable to others—augurs poorly for its objectivity.

A personal understanding is one that speaks to me. However, for a personal understanding to avoid being privatistic, it must be able to speak to another. It should be able to stand the light of day. If work is a social undertaking, something we do together, my colleagues should have some access to my own understanding of the meaning of what it is we are doing.

Notice that the characteristic "social" modifies the characteristic "experience based". Experience informs, but it can also narrow, confine, or delimit the one having the experience. Experience, furthermore, must be interpreted. But the act of interpreting uses more than personal experience for the interpretation. As we interpret our own experiences, we employ, with varying degrees of awareness, the interpretations of others—those of our colleagues, of the communities of which we were or are a part, of our education, and of our faith.

A personally composed, experience-based, social, and communicable spirituality is relevant for one who works because it influences one's attitude, motivation, choices, and the manner in which one works. If it has no relationship to the values of a community, it will not pass the test of objectivity.

Another characteristic of this theological reflection is that it must be critical. The antithesis of critical is *naive*. A naive theological reflection would be pious pap that uses religion to justify a situation it either ignored or was unable to critique. As we will explain at greater length in the next chapter, a critique must analyze the ideology that holds the work operation together. Every work operation has such an ideology.

An ideology can be examined either in terms of the various interests pursued by those engaged in the enterprise, or by becoming aware of the implicit assumptions made by those who shape the operation. Another way of understanding a workplace is in terms of power. Wherever people are, there is a distribution of power. Along with interests and assumptions, this distribution must be critically examined. To hide these universal dynamics under religious rhetoric would do a great disservice to truth, religion, oneself, and one's colleagues, not to mention the community that is supposedly being served by the productivity of the operation.

A thorough spirituality of work cannot ignore the larger, wider system within which the local work situation operates. This might be the industry itself or the local economy. Such analysis could also take into account the economic system itself, with its two primary dynamics of supply and demand.

But doesn't this task require more competence than any one person could possibly have? The answer is yes. Nonetheless the purpose in mentioning these wider matters is not to intimidate the reader but only to remind readers that they work within structures and that the more knowledge they can acquire about these structures, the more valuable the resultant spirituality will be to others, especially to other workers, and the more critical it will be.

Closely related to the characteristic of the critical is the issue of social analysis. To ask any in-depth question of the system—about such issues as workers' or consumers' rights, corporate responsibility, complicity in evil, or the common good—one would have to make explicit one's implicit and ever developing theories of society and the economy. We all have them, much as we might protest the opposite; they are shaped every morning by the newspaper and every night by the television. It can also be presumed that everyone has some analytical tools and a priori assumptions with which they critique their social reality.

In this matter of being critical and elaborating a critical spir-

ituality, it might of some value to note two different routes people
take in analyzing the social realities around them, and two different
views of social reality most people entertain. One view is functional.
It is highly pragmatic and works with a modicum of theory. It sees
the operative social forces in a given situation as poised in a fragile
equilibrium. When crises arise, those sympathetic to this func-
tionalist perspective anticipate that a return to the equilibrium can
be achieved. They will do their analysis on the basis of that optimism. They tend also to believe that the means for achieving this
restoration of equilibrium are already in place. (Those who entertain
this general view of society in a formal manner are reflecting the
functionalistic kind of social analysis once elaborated by Talcott
Parsons and other sociologists.)

The second view of society is more radical. It does not see society
as being in equilibrium. Those who pursue this kind of social analysis look for a profound change in the system. They are not interested
in fine-tuning the system, as the functionalists are. They are interested in eventually arriving at an equilibrium that has not heretofore
been achieved. Those who have this kind of attitude might be called
dialecticians, since they see two different forces locked in profound
conflict: the thesis is in place; they themselves represent the
antithesis; what has to emerge is a synthesis, or a new system.

Those who employ this second kind of social analysis are usually
on the bottom of the economy or, at least, prone to identify with
those on the bottom. In contrast, the functionalists who are prepared to fix something that is just a little bit broken are most often
the people who would fear any systemic changes since the present
arrangement is either tolerable or beneficial to them.

Two more characteristics of a spirituality of work are self-
explanatory: it must be dynamic and it must be theological. It is
inevitably dynamic because the particulars of any work situation are
always very much in flux. To try to fit last year's understanding to
this year's work scene will certainly produce a misreading of the
context. It is not that last year's understanding should be consigned
to the scrap heap but that the ever new situation within which work
is performed subjects the spirituality to ongoing re-envisioning.

By undertaking to compose your own spirituality of work, you as a
worker are not dealing with a matter that has fairly little variation in

data, as would be the case, for example, with a theology of Mary or a theology of the sacrament of confirmation. Since work as an object of theological reflection is part of an ever changing situation, it cannot be done once and for all.

It might be obvious to say that a spirituality of work must be theological, but there are several kinds of understandings that come close but fall short of being theological. One would be a social analysis that produced a sociology of work. Another would be an ethical analysis in which justice or injustice would be the focus. Or one could concentrate on the economics of the work situation. Or one could delight in some abstract vision and end up with a philosophy of work. But a spirituality of work must be about work as it is, and about God's interest in and relation to that work, insofar as one's sources give one access to that component of daily work.

## Spirituality and Childlikeness

Before concluding this chapter we need to return to the meaning of spirituality. It is a nebulous term. I will not define it since I do not believe it can or should be defined. But what it connotes needs to be confined lest it sprawl in too many directions to have any intelligibility at all.

Spirituality is a descriptive term, not a scientific term. It describes the relationship between the human spirit and the Holy Spirit, both of which are transcendental in scope. The Holy Spirit (along with the One whose Spirit it is) is ever at work on our aspirations, our interpretations, our choices, and would be effective in doing so if we permitted it full sway over us. Insofar as the human spirit allows the Holy Spirit access, a formal spirituality, in the theological sense of that term, develops. Otherwise, we operate out of an informal, pretheological spirituality, meaning that the human spirit stamps our actions, choices, and interpretations with whatever it independently construes as meaningful. Spirituality in the formal theological sense has one foot in the theoretical and one foot in the personal. If it were exclusively theoretical, it would not be distinguishable from spiritual theology. If it were only personal, it would be too idiosyncratic to elaborate.

A person's or a group's formal spirituality would have to be at least partly traditional because the Holy Spirit has been around for a long while and there are authentic, authenticated instances of the work of this Spirit. These instances can serve as benchmarks for measuring the present. The Spirit blows where it wills and moves on. Present ways of the Spirit must be in alignment with past workings. But past ways of working do not deny or disallow new ways of working. Benchmarks harken to a past and disclose continuity, but they do not call for imitation or conformity. So, an authentic, theological spirituality must be consciously rooted in the past, not to be mired there but to learn from it.

Anyone with even a smattering of knowledge of church history will appreciate how similar yet how different God's acts are in each generation of Christianity. Think of the earliest description of the community's spirituality in the Acts of the Apostles, where it is claimed that no one owned anything and that all things were shared in common on the basis of each one's needs (Acts 2:44–45). Not long after this, the conviction of martyrdom's great value was articulated.[6] Soon after that, self-denial and asceticism came to the fore, followed by the flight into the desert, the preservation of virginity, and eventually the vows of poverty, chastity, and obedience.[7] The popular devotions of the Middle Ages still affect our own modern Christian spirituality.

By recalling a few of these examples we are reminded of the evolutionary character of spirituality. The human spirit is never static. Its aspirations are for the infinite; its responses are always finite yet forever new. Without knowledge of and reverence for the past, we proceed into the future underequipped for the task at hand.

I would locate spirituality even more specifically in what Paul Ricoeur calls "the science of the individual."[8] If that is the right category in which to locate it, as I believe it is, then its verification by a series of scientific probes is beside the point. One's spirituality is much more a matter of interpretation than verification. Granted, interpretation must be valid, but the process of validation is ongoing and interactive. The interaction is between the person and the present community, both the working community and the believing community. It is also between the person and the tradition of spirituality that shows itself in sacred texts.

Infrequently, spiritualities of individuals have been validated or verified. When they are, the spirituality in question becomes "a science of the many," to twist Ricoeur's phrase. This has occurred in the church's canonization of those who lived an understanding of the Gospels and left a record of their understanding for posterity.

Finally, childlikeness must be commented upon, since it more than any other quality is required for the successful completion of the task before us. To know God even ever so slightly is to know that one is a child. In fact, one can be only a child before God, before whom there are only children. In understanding God or the things of God or the things of the world on God's own terms, the childlike Christian knows his or her need for God: God begins the good work and brings it to completion. If each of us is wholly dependent on God's help and grace in responding to everyday challenges, how much more are we in need of God for the development of a new dimension to our union with God. At no point in the process does one become a pro. There are no pros in God's eyes, only faithful and unfaithful children. Only children make it into the Kingdom of God. And anyone seeking growth in this kingdom will require growth in childlikeness.

So far, the characteristics of a spirituality of work are that it be personally composed, experience based, personal but accessible through its use of publically available documents, social, critical, personally relevant, traditional, dynamic, and theological. This list alone could be overwhelming to novice composers. To persevere in doing what we are recommending in this volume, the composer will have to proceed with an attitude of childlikeness. A child is undaunted by the complexity of things. But the complexity of what we are attempting is daunting to adults. That may be why "professionals" don't ordinarily undertake to compose such a thing. Professionals can assist us along the way in coming to a spirituality. But eventually we are each on our own. One does not have to gain a professional's permission to proceed in interpreting the data and living one's faith.

# 9

# A Method

Recall from the previous chapter that the proposed effort is to be done largely by the reader. How, in God's name, can it succeed? the reader might be wondering at this point. This chapter will attempt to remove some of the mystification by relating the process to the real workaday world and by recommending a method, a way of proceeding—a methodology, if you please.

This chapter spells out a usable method for ordinary people who seek to grow religiously in the course of working at their respective jobs. It is *a* method, not *the* method. When it comes to spirituality, which is a science of the individual, as I have called it, we are dealing with something that is too personal and idiosyncratic an undertaking to presume that there is only one method to satisfy all mentalities.

One of the values of any method is that it helps one avoid relying too much on intuition. Discrete steps, each distinct from the others, keep us from mental meandering or from becoming confused. A well-conceived method can keep its user from developing or falling back into sloppy intellectual habits. Many of the following steps might emerge naturally for some people, but that is not certain. Leaving out even just one step jeopardizes the entire effort.

In the steps we will recommend there is a natural flow that will resolve some of seeming contradictions in the characteristics described in the first chapter. Some of these characteristics may seem mutually exclusive: for example, relevant yet traditional, personal yet social, and experienced based yet developed from publicly accessible documents.

The idea of methodology evokes very diverse responses. Some people have a natural aversion to methods. They fear that methods

138

will constrict them or constrain their spontaneity. Other people
have a natural attraction to methods. (They are likely to be "J-type"
personalities in the Myers-Briggs categories of perception prefer-
ences.) Some of these latter people could be called "technoholics":
they love to be furnished with methods so that they can feel more
secure about "getting it right" or "doing it right," thereby ensuring
success in their projects.

The value of the method proposed here is its ability to unleash
creativity and imagination where appropriate and yet be structured
and pragmatic at the same time. Both groups—those with an attraction and those with an aversion—can be assisted by the proposed
method. Careful inclusion of each step will make it more likely that
the effort will be successful.

Not only does this method have a natural flow but it will not be
wholly unfamiliar to users since it will take what is ordinarily implicit in their discernment of their responsibilities and make it
explicit. The method spelled out here can be used in a thorough
fashion over a long period of time, or it can be abridged and used in
an abbreviated manner, lightly. The more thorough approach is
called for in the beginning of the process of one's religious reflection
on work. In time, the steps in the process can become second
nature.

The object of one's reflection may be very specific, such as an
immediate problem that has developed in the workplace, or it may
be as broad as one's whole experience of a given job. The broader
the scope, the more formal and thorough the use of the method
should be.

Finally, the method can be used by individuals or, even better, by
small groups, preferably in the same work situation, profession, or
industry. As has already been mentioned in the first chapter, there is
a precedent for this small-group approach in the more than one
hundred thousand base communities in Latin America. The sim-
ilarities between what they are doing and what is being proposed
here is a desire to integrate faith and life and a method for doing so.
The dissimilarities also have to do with method—theirs is not ours—
and with culture and economic conditions. Furthermore, our interest is more narrow, namely, faith and work. I merely cite these base
communities here to encourage the reader to think in terms of a

small-group use of the following method, and to observe that dramatic changes can take place when there is a felt need for change (as these base communities can attest).

## The Steps

### 1. The Naming Step

In the first step, the person or group attempts to move from inattentiveness to attentiveness about their work situation, from indistinct impressions to more definite perceptions. The awareness here focuses on the component parts of the work situation: for example, the physical circumstances, the psychological context, or the objectives being pursued and the policies devised to pursue them. Inevitably, however, the people—their responsibilities and roles, how they interact with one another and the networks among them—will ordinarily be the most important components of the work scene.

It is not necessary here to be analytic or exhaustive. The more important result of this first step is that feelings begin to surface in the reviewer(s) during the course of the review. Reviewers should take seriously their attractions and aversions, satisfactions and dissatisfactions, and begin to name these. As a result, the relevant pieces of the work situation will be out on the table, and one's own angle of vision will become more explicit.

Used in a group, this first step will be similar to composing a story out of the shared impressions of each of the people who come together for the exercise. The purpose of the step is not to make judgments about the corporation or other people, but to become aware of their impact, noting especially their effects on each participant in the exercise. If this qualification is not understood, this first step can result in an indictment of absent parties, which would be as far from the spirit of composing a spirituality as one can get.

This first step is based in what is sometimes called "thinking with the right side of the brain." It seeks to get a sense of the whole, and to do so more intuitively than analytically. Feelings and impressions are taken seriously.

Obviously, this is a good start, but the process cannot stop here.

## 2. The Decoding Step

The impressions and feeings that surfaced in the first step must now be subjected to a deeper reading. The second step is called "decoding" because each person's job in the workplace comes to him or her already in code. Coding means an interpretation has already been given to the job and the context within which it is performed. The employee never enters a vacuum but is brought into a social context that is filled with much more than just people working at their respective job descriptions. Every employee and employer, furthermore, brings much more than their own skills to the workplace. They bring their own needs, assumptions, purposes, motivations, and interests. These will not be clear, especially at first, but it is largely from these needs, assumptions, purposes, and interests, that the coding is woven into the fabric of the workplace.

Those who would construct a spirituality of work for themselves must recognize that a kind of "spirituality of work" is already operating in their work situation. This spirituality is the sum total of the ways those who work at the same operation react to the "givens" circumscribing them. These givens are the conditions and circumstances people find themselves in at work, plus the tasks to be done. The human spirit is not ordinarily willing to be shapcd by such givens. How the personnel in a particular work situation manipulate or attempt to shape what is given creates the particular unexamined "spirituality" that is already operating. This unexamined spirituality is synonymous with the coding operating in a particular workplace.

Decoding first requires social analysis, and then judgment. Recall the distinction made in the previous chapter about social analysis. Its two forms are either functional or dialectical. In its functional form social analysis is undertaken to bring the dysfunctional back into equilibrium. In its dialectical form, social analysis is done with a view to changing the system. Whichever level of analysis one undertakes, one will find that three closely related dynamics hold the key to successful decoding: interests, ideology, and power. One can uncover the unexamined "spirituality"—which is to say, break the code—by analysis of these three social dynamics in any work situation. Interests are more difficult to grasp than motivations or purposes, although they are all interrelated. *Motives* are why you do the work you do. Like purposes, motives are conscious and appear to be straightforward. *Interests*, on the other hand, are whatever it is one gets or is trying to get out of the work one does. Interests are usually unstated, even to oneself. They are more likely to be revealed in one's actions than by the words we tell ourselves or others.

One's own interests and those operating at the workplace must be uncovered and evaluated since, having developed in the course of the period of employment, they will have at least as much impact on the dynamics of the workplace as does the work itself. The interests that are uncovered must be evaluated according to one's more considered values. The interests might be morally neutral, but this cannot be presumed. It is much more likely that the interests will be morally freighted: they will either be good, meaning they will be concerned with doing good work and with the good of the work done for others, or they will be morally deficient.

Some of the many interests operating in a workplace are the desires for recognition, security, and position. (These are related to value drives, that were examined in chapter 1. These drives are those for mastery, information, meaning, survival, relatedness, pleasure, dignity, and play.)

An immoral interest would be unusual among readers of this volume. The more frequent deficiency will lie in the range of interest being too narrow, in not extending beyond oneself or "one's own." An interest is deficient when it ignores the social potential of work and its impact on others. We will assume, therefore, that people interested in spirituality of work will be oriented toward the good of others and will aspire to go beyond mere self-interest.

Another useful rubric for this decoding step is to see the work site in terms of the ideology that operates in it. Everyone knows more or less what an ideology is: it is a world view; here, it is a posture taken toward the employer, customer, system, business competition, or government. The ideology of any work site is for the most part the sum total of the interests that succeed in shaping the workplace to operate as it does. The adjective *dominant*, therefore, is a clarifying qualifier of *ideology*. The effect the dominant ideology has on the work force is that it justifies the interests of those involved, leaving them with the feeling that "this is the way things are done here." It is the accepted modus operandi.

The comment that was made above about the relationship between interests and motives also applies here: one is not likely to find the actual ideology of a company in its mission statement or in its stated objectives. Rather, ideology becomes evident in the day-to-day operation of the company itself. More important than what a business says about itself is what it really does in practice. Some of the important behaviors that reveal the ideology of a given business are the assumptions it accepts, the practices it chooses to ignore, and the practices it chooses to punish, the anxieties it entertains, the actions it rewards or punishes in its employees, its treatment of the consumer and the community, its attitude toward the larger systems of which it is a part, and its wage scales (especially in relation to its profits). The employees know the actual ideology even though it is largely unspoken and never written. No employee, whether management or nonmanagement, can ignore or be indifferent to this ideology. One is either for it and acquiescent to it (and therefore a reinforcer of it) or against it (although most opposition is usually covert). The dominant ideology can be sensitive to people or to the bottom line. It can be competitive to the point of being combative or competitive but also aware of people. It can be hypocritical, talking a good game to the gullible public, or direct and forthright in its dealings with the public. It can be predatory and greedy, or oriented toward service and community. The possibilities are endless.

Part of the decoding step is judging the behavior it uncovers. If the behavior is reprehensible one must be careful "to judge the sin and not the sinner" because, as we mentioned before, the purpose of the exercise is not to issue indictments but to develop a response to one's work environment that is worthy of the name Christian spirituality.

The very fact that one attempts this decoding indicates that one refuses to accept what is ordinarily taken for granted by the rest of the work force, namely, that the way things are is the way they have to be. After reviewing the primary interests that hold the operation together, one might end up largely in agreement with the operative ideology, or one might reject the ideology. The desired outcome of the whole exercise is to become much more selective about the ideology that one either accepts and reinforces or eschews and combats. Whichever direction one takes, the point is that in every social situation and, therefore, in every work situation, the dominant ideology, as the sum total of the interests involved, tends to make it what it is.

A third useful rubric for decoding the work situation is that of power and how it is distributed. Every social situation is a distribution of power. This is certainly the case in the work context. The distribution might be perceived as good for all those in the situation as well as for those outside of it who are impacted by it. But this cannot be presumed and the situation must be reviewed with the distribution of power as a key object of reflection.

Like the other two objects of reflection, power could be analyzed endlessly. But the analysis must be practical, and pertinent to matters that surfaced in the first step. One would be hopelessly frustrated if an equal distribution of power by all parties were envisioned or desired. Nonetheless, the presence or absence of power to participate is a key to unlocking areas of job satisfaction and dissatisfaction. When power is justly distributed all parties are accorded the power to be participants, not merely recipients of someone else's commands. Participation is the power to be heard, to have some influence on the modus operandi of the workplace by having a voice.

An elaboration of all the other dimensions of power would take us too far afield. Suffice it to say at this point that employees know when there is a real abuse of power, an unjust arrogation of power, or an absence of structures for its distribution. If any of these situations have surfaced, the decoding step must deal with them by identifying operative self-interests and the operative ideology that enables the situation to exist.

## 3. The Faith Lens

The strengths of the first two steps are the strengths of perception versus oblivion, judgment versus impressions, the critical versus the uncritical, the explicit versus the implicit, and the reflective versus the taken for granted. So far, however, our steps have not touched religious faith or the norms faith furnishes for our judgments. If we wish to compose a spirituality of work, our judgments and critical attitudes must be based in faith and the data we judge must be judged through the lens of faith and theology. We need a step in which the lens through which we judge the data is cleansed. Hence the need for this third step, the development of a faith lens.

The religious faith of the worker might have been operative in the first and second steps. If it was, this step will make it more reflective and explicit. If it was not, this step will formally introduce faith into the process of reflection. This can happen in several ways.

### Discovery and Magnification

Some of what is already on the table from the first two steps will be seen as having clear moral implications: hatred, greed, anger, lust, jealousy, envy, injustice, or dishonesty may have come to the surface. This evidence must be dealt with in terms of one's faith. The observer's angle of vision on a moral issue might be that of victim or guilty sinner or complicit participant. Whichever, it is clear that God would enter into this matter directly. Repentance, confrontation, and whistle blowing would be three of our more frequent responses to patently moral matters.

God can also be discoverd to be at work in manifest instances of virtue, such as honesty, kindness, courage, and any other moral virtue operating in the people with whom one works. God can be discovered, therefore, either where there is a great need for God because there is notable moral deficiency, or where the work of God in people is pronounced. In either case there will be a still small voice that has to be amplified.

A few examples may suffice here: an uneasy feeling that a product isn't being made correctly for the consumer or a service that the customer has a right to have done isn't being performed. Such feelings are rightly made the object of explicit attention. On the other hand, an appreciation of the service character of the work I do, or that we as a firm do for others, can be freshly appropriated. Or an antipathy to management can develop in one who perceives an unfairness because of excessive slackness by oneself or one's colleagues. Other examples are a feeling of going through the motions in a company that evokes no loyalty; a feeling of meaninglessness because the company has been merged or acquired by absentee owners; a relational impasse between people who distrust one another; a sense of becoming obsolete because of imminent changes in technology; a profound distrust of the industry or the profession of which my work is a part; gross mistreatment of an employee by the company; blatant sexism, racism, or any other discrimination in hiring or promotion practices. These are some of the negative situations employers and employees face regularly.

Any of these situations might have already been subjected to judgment in either of the first two steps. The point of the third step is to examine the situation in and through the eyes of one's faith. This examination might require only a greater degree of attention to see God at work in it or God's will about it. When the matter has not been clarified by giving it attention, more clarity will be needed about some of the facts or about the norm needed to judge it. In the latter case, religious ideals, church doctrines, Gospel norms, or some other teachings of one's faith will have to surface to supply the criteria by which the matter under review is interpreted or reinterpreted. What might have been a still small voice in the first steps now needs to become a word commanding one's attention. The word can and hopefully will grow into an understanding of the faith response to the work situation.

This step in the process is one of magnification, since there is a need for the Lord to be magnified. One's faith has brought us to focus attention on some particular situation. As a consequence, the need for God or God's working is given much more attention than is ordinarily the case. My soul and mind and heart magnify the Lord! (We have taken a longer look at ways of finding God in the ordinary things of one's work life in chapter 4.)

## Contemplation and Theology

Countless associations with work situations have convinced me that few people expect to find God at work or regularly experience God at work. Furthermore, theological reflection on one's work is infrequent while the habitual way of viewing one's work is almost universally secular. Given the fact that even actively Christian people tend to be unaware of how or even whether to reflect on their jobs in terms of their faith, the need for contemplation and theological reflection is usually more pressing than the need for discovery and magnification. The more desirable way, of course, for the faith dimension to emerge in our process is to find God at work. But a direct infusion of theological or religious data may first be necessary for this third step to be successful.

When it is not evident how God is present in the work situation, it is best to temporarily suspend what has surfaced in the first and second steps. What must be pursued at this point is the development of a clearer faith horizon, one suited to the situation. This faith horizon must be clear and sufficiently vivid to embrace the work situation that has been seen in steps one and two. Our faith must be strong enough and the horizon vital enough that the insertion of the data from these first two steps causes us to reinterpret what we have seen so that we can see things from a new angle of vision.

Our religious horizon can become vital and vivid through theological reflection or prayerful reflection on a biblical symbol or story or theme or image. We would have to presume some familiarity with the Scriptures; one passage or theme rather than another would be selected because it seemed more promising for enlightening us about the matter that surfaced in the first steps. (The previous chapters have provided a selection of both scriptural texts and themes to enlighten work and some of the myriad situations that develop at work.)

There are many ways in which one's faith horizon can come alive. An effective liturgy or a pointed homily, a passage from one's reading, an event in one's life that brings one up short, or a mind-blowing conversation that forces one to reflect—these are the kinds of things that can cause unexpected changes in one's horizon. If one doesn't have the good fortune to experience such things in the course of daily life, one must go out and look for them.

Whether through magnification or theology, the purpose of this third step is to see one's work in a new light. "For one who is in Christ, he/she is a new creation; the old order has passed away" (2 Cor. 5: 17). Christians should expect this newness and seek it out. Until this step is taken we are still short of a spirituality of work in the formal sense.

### 4. The Encoding Step

The encoding step flows naturally from the previous ones. Presumably, new insight has been gained from the first three steps.

Presumably, too, it is now clear that a new coding must be given to the work situation since the old code has probably not been able to bear the weight of analysis and the explicit entry of God into the situation. I must reinterpret my work (or we must reinterpret our work) on the basis of what has been understood, especially from the third step—this is the task of encoding. A new ideology, if we may call it such, one based in a better understanding of God's revelation, must be completed by seeing the implications of what has been understood so far for the actual, everyday work scene. Perhaps a better image is that of the new wine that has been produced in the exercise up to this point: here new wineskins are needed to contain this new wine so that it can be used to our satisfaction.

If the third step was done with care and with the help of God's grace, which should be explicitly petitioned, then God has already begun to break into the scene. The encoding step will try to fit one's new angle of vision to situations one has already faced innumerable times. This is tricky and takes much discretion. Even more, the gift of discernment is needed: this is an art that needs the Spirit's gift of "discernment of spirits." There will always be two "spirits" at work and they will invariably be in conflict with one another. One of these is the Spirit of God, the other is the spirit embodied in the ideology of the workplace. This later will always be in need of conversion to the common good.

The encoding step must be done prayerfully since it necessitates a discernment of the relationship between the actual and the desirable. Our awareness of this relationship develops out of a new understanding of God's interests, God's "ideology," and God's power via-à-vis the interests, the ideology, and the powers already in place. In most work situations, the disparity between the actual and the desirable is considerable.

## 5. The Resolution Step

The first four steps must now evolve into a process of concrete planning and execution. *Praxis* is work done on the basis of a new perception of work's meaning. The new praxis will be undertaken on the basis of the discernment that has been made. Praxis is work done with theory that is developed from experience, in this case, the experience of the work site.[1] It is work done with an understanding of what is called for by the work situation and a faith response to it. In many respects a spirituality of work is an exercise in holy politics since there may be political difficulties as one returns to the work scene with a different angle of vision from which new actions and new attitudes will spring.

The new praxis will not take place in a vacuum. It will evoke responses since it will differ from the workers' previous actions. Anticipating the responses and weighing one's resolve according to the expected reactions is a part of what this step involves.

## Reflections on the Process

Where does this method come from? It has a kinship with several other methods of reflection, among them the Prayer of the Examen recommended in the Spiritual Exercises of Saint Ignatius. The insight behind this prayer is that God is at work in our affections. The person using this method of prayer examines God working in him or her by a regular review (as often as once or twice a day) of these affective nudges. Ignatius called them consolations or desolations depending on whether they nudged the person toward God and toward doing the will of God or away from God and toward that which distances one from God.[2]

This prayer corresponds to the first part of the third step in our method: "discovery and magnification." It is strongly recommended by Ignatius because his own experience was that God is at work in our lives much more fully than we realize and that this prayer heightened one's awareness. Some of the important things that are done to and for us by God can happen while we remain oblivious but can be caught after the fact by this prayer form. This discovery can create a horizon by focusing attention on the moment and on the word that emerges from this focused attention.

A second forerunner of this method is the "see-judge-act" method that was widely used in Europe before and after World War II. It was used first by the Jocists, a movement that was also called the Young Christian Workers. Their Belgian founder and mentor, Monsignor Joseph Cardijn, was the author of the formula. The Jocist movement was composed of cells of young workers who sought a deeper form of faith. Their practice was to come together with regularity and submit themselves to a process in which the first step was *seeing* their situation in all its particulars. Seeing involved two foci, one "temporal," the other "eternal." The second step was *judging*. This also was bifocal, both "temporal" and "eternal." The third step was *acting* "with a view to the conquest of their [the Jocists'] eternal and temporal destiny."[3]

In the mid-1950s the Jocists claimed to have one and one-half million members in sixty-four different countries. One can catch the flavor of Cardijn's vigor in one of his elaborations on the action part of the formula: workers are to

> Act—individually and collectively, in a team, in a local section, in a regional federation, in a national movement, in meetings, in achievement, in life and in their environment, forming a single front, going forward to the conquest of the masses of their fellow workers.[4]

Valuable as it was, it is somewhat dated now, both sociologically and theologically. Theologically it tended to dichotomize the natural and the supernatural, the temporal and the eternal. It had "zeal for souls" a zeal that saw nothing but evil and danger in the faith in Marxism and socialism. It did not flourish beyond the time of the Second Vatican Council.

A third forerunner of the method we have elaborated is the process of reflection that comes out of liberation theology. We have already mentioned that the Latin American context in which this process was developed is one of enormous disparity between rich and poor, with the poor being the overwhelming majority. A dialectical kind of social analysis, therefore, was and is inevitable in this context. The method used by the base communities seeks a radical change in the economic and political systems, not a return to equilibrium (as is the case with a functional social analysis).

The base communities use a dialectical process of reflection in which the two parts of the dialectic are called *revolutionary praxis* and *critical theory*.[5] Work becomes praxis when it is undergirded by meaning and theory. Meaningless work is work that is done in an alienated manner. The alienation in the case of the Latin American poor does not arise merely from their working conditions. They were and are marginalized by the entire economic and political system in which they live and work.

Revolutionary praxis, work done from meaning, is undertaken with an understanding of how things are, can be and ought to be. It is done with a view toward needed changes in the conditions of work and, in turn, of the conditions of society. The meaning the worker takes to work and finds in work derives from the base community's reflection on their work and life experiences. The fruit of their reflection they call critical theory. It is critical because they have no naiveté about the system within which they work. It is theory because they have come to a consciousness about how the system operates and how it could and should work given their dignity as persons. Together they plumb the Scriptures, which are a major source of their theory.

This method has many variations and many authors. It owes much to Latin American social theorists. Paulo Freire, a Brazilian educator, developed an important piece of the method with his insight into consciousness raising through reflection on praxis.[6]

The base-community movement has not caught on in North America. For one thing, it would appear that it thrives in a social context of enormous economic disparity and political unrest. It also presumes there is a people hungering for community. The individualism of North Americans and their middle-class economic status keeps this kind of movement south of the border. There would have to be a sense of urgency about radical social change to make both their method and their movement attractive.

There is a fourth forerunner of this method. Like the other three it has been catalytic for many theologians and pastoral experts. It is the self-conscious development of religious education as a discipline in its own right. Religious education had long been the messenger boy delivering the considered judgments of the church's magisterium and the theological reflections of the scholarly community to the people. This made both the educators and their pupils receptacles of truths. Today this is seen as neither good education nor good theology.

Good theology is ever developing. Its ongoing development must include a hearing of those who practice and reflect on their own faith. The informal reflective wisdom that comes from the lived faith of the Christian community both informs and forms the theologian. Good theology is done by hearts as well as heads. Once formation of the heart ceases, theology usually becomes an exercise in cogitation. The truths of the faith come from the mysteries of God and Christ. Their celebration by the faithful as participants is the raw material of good theology. All must walk the way of faith to reflect on it credibly. Faith is a truth that all know in varying degrees; it is a life that admits of many levels of participation. The old paradigm in which truth comes from knowers to the ignorant is yielding to a more sophisticated insight that sees lived faith as informing even while it is being informed.

The process of coming to know the faith is a specialization in itself, one that involves much activity on the part of the would-be learner. It also usually involves community, and training in the sharing of one's faith and faith experience. One of the better mentors in this process is Thomas Groome, whose book *Christian Religious Educators* is helpful to our understanding of both the development of religious education and its method (a method that in some respects mirrors the method described in this chapter).[7]

## How the Method Relates to Theology and Ethics

The effort to understand God and faith has been pursued since time immemorial. It has been undertaken formally by theologians and informally by the rest of believers. When the effort functioned as it was intended, both of these populations needed and fed one another: the practice and informal reflection developed a *sensus fidelium,* (a "sense of faith of the faithful") that was and is "the activity of reflective wisdom in the believer."[8]

Our intent in this book is to bring a method to bear on the informal process of understanding faith. The informal can be made more systematic without having to become formal theology. Just as the narrow definition of ministry is being broadened, so also the preserve of theology is being widened to include all who pursue this activity of reflective wisdom. The method outlined here differs from formal theology in terms of its objects of reflection: here these

objects are the situations one finds oneself in in the world, specifically, one's work situation as an object looked at by means of the light
of faith for that situation.

Professor Edward Farley of Vanderbilt's School of Divinity has
developed the helpful category of "the situation of the believer."[9]
Traditional theology has seen its task as that of interpreting the faith
of the believer so that people could apply its interpretations to their
practices, interior needs, or ecclesial behavior. "The problem with
this paradigm is that it bypasses most of the structural elements in
the situation of the believer and, therefore, many other interpretive
acts."[10] Farley complains that the bulk of theological effort has
concentrated on interpreting texts and has had little interest in
interpreting the situations in which the faith is operating or would
operate.[11]

Theology has traditionally moved "from a disciplined interpretation of the authoritative past to a casual and impressionistic grasp of
the present."[12] This encourages an obliviousness to one's context,
which does justice neither to faith nor to the situation. Furthermore, only from a very narrow understanding of God, faith, and the
situation could one assume God to be absent from the situation
unless brought there by the believer. It is not our faith that brings
God to the situation; it is our faith that interprets how God is already
operating in the situation and would operate with greater freedom in
it through reflective believers.

The situations in which we find ourselves are theologically significant. Recall that faith has been and still is mediated to us through
determinate, specific situations. It does not come unmediated out of
the blue. "Faith comes through hearing" (Rom. 10:17), hearing what
is being said through people in situations or through the situations
themselves. The still small voice that would speak to us speaks
through highly ambiguous and localized circumstances. The word
one hears in one's conscience or heart is spoken in and through a
context. To interpret a word independently of its context is like
interpreting a word independently of the text within which it is
found. This is a good way to misinterpret the word.

To be in a long-term work situation without a method of reflection
on one's faith is a disservice to oneself, one's faith, and one's colleagues. It makes it virtually certain that an areligious meaning is

being assigned to what is being done. This inevitably misinforms all parties—both believers and their colleagues.

If we stop assuming that the only thing that needs to be critically interpreted is the text which carries the faith's meaning, we will come to see the importance of the interpretation of the context within which the faith is lived out. There must be a self-conscious, self-critical, and disciplined interpretation of the situation itself. An uninterpreted work context functions as a secularized world view without our being aware that this is the case or that it is malfunctioning. Such a world view both coarsens our sensitivity to spiritual things and heightens our sensitivity to other things, usually those that represent, trigger, or threaten our particular self-interest. Critically assessing the world view through which we filter all the phenomena of the work situation requires a decoding of the operative ideology. This is necessary for the new choices and actions that will develop as we view our work situation through a cleansed lens.

A thorough decoding must go in several directions, one of these being into the past and the other in greater depth into the present. The first of these decoding directions, toward past conditions and their causes, is needed to understand the problems that have surfaced in the present situation. Present distortions or repressions can at times be uncovered only by knowledge of forgotten culprits or causes. The second direction is toward present functionings of the economy in all its relevant parts. This direction is not optional; it will always be necessary to a greater or lesser degree. The wider business and financial picture of the American economy must be examined in order to attain to a better understanding of most of the local work phenomena. Shifts and pressures and crises at the work site seldom develop in isolation from the fast-moving changes of capitalism and the dynamics of modern business. This does not mean that we noneconomists must become economists in order to undertake a spirituality of work; it is not a call for crash courses in political science, philosophy, or sociology. Rather, it is a call for awareness of the fact that structural and systemic pressures shape the local work situation.

Although there is some overlap between a spirituality of work and an ethics of work, it is nonetheless helpful to distinguish one from the other. Both ethics and spirituality are concerned with behavior, in this case, work-related behavior. An ethics of the workplace is ordinarily concerned with the conditions within which work is done and the norms needed to bring integrity to those conditions. A spirituality of work is not unconcerned with these issues, but it is more wholistic and personal. It is focused more on the character and "work ethic of the worker" than on the ethical conditions of the workplace. A spirituality of work is also focused on the religious foundations of the workers' behavior, whereas an ethics of the workplace seeks norms to regulate workplace conditions. More often than not, a failure in the integrity of the workers is not due to an absence of norms or an ignorance of what constitutes right behavior. Rather, it is due to a failure of the will, and an insufficient desire to pursue what is known to be the right course of action or to desist from wrong actions. Granted, there will be times when the lens that is needed is an ethical one, and clarity will be needed in regard to norm for right actions. But this will not happen often.

Catholic social doctrine as developed by the magisterium in the last one hundred years is a rich trove of ethical principles relevant to work. These principles deserve a whole separate study. Useful as they are for an ethics of the workplace, however, they are less helpful in developing a spirituality. Furthermore, these principles too often ask people to run before they have learned to walk. By developing a personal understanding of the religious dimension of their work, workers are more likely to come to a concern about work conditions and the transformation of the workplace. A spirituality of work, while it will be concerned with changing the ethical climate of the workplace, is first concerned with what is usually prior to ethics, namely, a consciousness of the religious meaning of the enterprise. Consciousness needs a method for getting hold of what is usually already latent in the interiority and faith of Christian persons. The successful method enables what is often already there to become conscious and operative.

Difficult work situations are created by human actions, and benign work situations can also be established by moral agency. Dismantling the inhumane and creating a good work situation requires both spirituality and ethics. Of the two, many more resources exist for those looking for ethical norms than for those looking to come to a new level of interiority with respect to their work. At the same time, it seems to me, there is much more need and desire for the process I call spirituality than for the one called ethics, even though this need is seldom named. It is not named because it has been so infrequently attempted that it is largely unknown.

There is too great a distance between academic theology and ethics and the ongoing practice of the faith in faith communities. More enlightened judgments, both theological and workaday, can come from a closer connection between the two. Faith becomes itself at those moments when the appropriated tradition touches the actual situation as it is perceived. A spirituality of work is intended to equip users with the means to reflect critically on both their own perception of their situation and their own faith.

Ethics, theology, and spirituality are three interpenetrating fields of reflection that should not be severed from one another. Each needs the others. Spirituality needs ethics and theology to avoid subjectivism. Both ethics and theology need spirituality to avoid formalism and abstraction. Theology, which has many specializations, generally seeks to know more about God and our interpretation of God. Ethics, which also has different specializations, generally seeks to know more about the good to be done and the evil to be avoided and what can be known objectively about these. Spirituality, which is too close to the "science of the individual" to be specialized, is first and foremost a response to God in love and service and only secondarily a reflection on this. It is comfortable with the kinds of questions Saint Ignatius posed for himself: "What have I done for Christ, what am I doing for Christ, and what shall I do for Christ?" Theology is more interested in examining who the Christ is for whom we do the things we do, and ethics is more interested in identifying the right things to do. Spirituality asks, What kind of person shall I be? Ethics asks, What ought to be done?

## Who Benefits from a Spirituality of Work?

For whom is this spirituality intended? How can it escape being narcissistic? It is obviously meant for faithful person or persons at work. But because it is grounded in a transcendent understanding of human dignity, it is also intended for all those who will be affected by the behavioral changes that result from the new understanding. By seeking to enlarge the scope of freedom and of justice for those who use the method, we also seek to enlarge freedom and justice for all parties. The same can be said about the self-determination and participation that are essential to human dignity. The Good News that is appropriated by believers is meant to be shared by them through word and deed so that others can be reminded of and reinforced in their dignity. All people were made in the image and likeness of God. All deserve a chance to experience their dignity by living and working in conditions that respect their status.

Anyone who has worked can testify that modern work situations often denigrate human dignity. The work situation can be corrupting or compromising—the possibilities for this are limitless. Sex and race discrimination, unjust wages, impossible working conditions, ridicule for attempting to be principled, bottom-line adherence that ignores human needs, fraud, embezzlement, sloth, dishonesty, open immorality, morale problems, sexual harassment—the list is endless. These situations rob persons of the truth of their transcendent dignity.

Truth makes all freer; untruth leaves all parties unfree. One cannot enter into a spirituality of work and remain unconcerned with the condition of one's colleagues. As we will see, there is an agenda that accompanies a spirituality of work, an agenda that Christ himself sought to perform in his ministry. Like him, we as his worker-followers should be concerned with serving our colleagues so that together we all can grow in our humanity to a fullness that transcends the work and actions we undertake together.

# Study Guide

The following questions and comments could serve as a review to the chapters. They do not pretend to touch on all the matter covered in the chapters. Instead they could be best used as conversation starters for groups using the book or goads to an individual's memory after the chapter was read, or to generate interest before reading it.

## Chapter 1 / Meaning and Work

1. Is your work meaningful? If it is, what makes it so?
2. Is it meaningful in an immanent sense or in a transcendent sense or both?
3. Do any of Maccoby's categories describe you? Have you graduated from the "partial man" theories of work motivation?
4. If your work is meaningless is the problem in your eye or in the objective situation objectively considered?
5. Which of the categories that hint at your work's transcendent meaning is most appealing to you? Could you elaborate on its relevance to you?

## Chapter 2 / The Creator God and Working People

1. Are you aware that you are making yourself by the work you are doing and by the manner of your doing it?
2. People are ever so subtly in the process of making themselves according to some image they have of what they might become or are meant to become. Are you aware of this in yourself?

3. Does the image and likeness of the God of Genesis 1 give you any image of who you are or are meant to be?
4. Does it give you any understanding of your dignity as worker?
5. What practical meaning does the vocation to have dominion have for you in your present work situation?
6. Do either alienation or domination play any part in your attitudes about your job or how you go about doing it? Do you see them functioning in your co-workers?

## Chapter 3 / Work and Rest

1. Have you developed the habit of sabbath?
2. If so, how do you succeed in achieving its refreshment of spirit?
3. Does the notion of counterfeit sabbath, or an immersion in distractions, describe your "day off" better than sabbath?
4. What are the implications for our practice of sabbath if Jesus subsumed the role of sabbath into himself?
5. If you do not experience sabbath in some degree, what are the obstacles impeding this?

## Chapter 4 / The God Who Works

1. Are you accustomed to find God in your work situation?
2. Which of the three sources or models for finding God at work are most helpful to your developing a habit in this matter?
3. Has the experience of discovering God in your work resulted in or produced "devotion" in you?
4. Do you see the whole enterprise at which you work in terms of God, e.g., God's interests, will, intentions; Christ's mission in the world? How do these interests show up in your day-to-day work?
5. Does the notion of covenant supply a foundational image for understanding your work and God's interest in its execution?

## Chapter 5 / Evil at Work

1. Does your workplace give you the feeling that God is absent from it?

2. Is its atmosphere one of indifference to God? Is there a covert assumption in the work force that religious faith is irrelevant to the enterprise as a whole? or an implicit belief that religion is irrelevant to us here?
3. Do you sense anything evil operating in the place, above and beyond the usual sins of individuals?
4. If so, can you describe the nature of that evil in any way? Does it appear to have a life of its own, or is it more simply explained as the sum total of everyone's moral failings?
5. Does it seem like it can be isolated and overcome or does it seem too pervasive and, therefore, invincible?

## Chapter 6 / What Work Lasts?

1. Is eschatology in the way it is described here a new way of thinking for you?
2. Could you describe the relevance to yourself of the question asked in this chapter?
3. Which of the texts of Scripture make the most sense to you in attempting to answer the question of work's dignity?
4. Which of the authors treated in the last section of the chapter bring the most light to the question?
5. What do you think will last of what you presently do?

## Chapter 7 / The Meaning God Sees

1. There are three steps in the anthropology of entrustment described here. Are any of them already in your spiritual repertoire? Are any of them repugnant or irrelevant to you?
2. Does the idea that your work can glorify God motivate you?
3. What would have to change in the manner of, and the motive for, working if working for the glory of God began to shape your sense of its meaning?

## Chapter 8 / A Spirituality of Work

Even before religious faith enters into the conversation, it could be helpful for readers to take a personal inventory with questions such as the following:

1. What is your work doing to you?
2. Are you happy with the kind of person your job is making you become?
3. Do you feel the need to situate your work onto the horizons of your faith?
4. How does your religious faith presently affect your view of your job? Your handling of or conduct on your job?
5. Conversely, how is your job affecting your faith?

## Chapter 9 / A Method

1. Do you see or feel the need for a method in undertaking this process?
2. Which of the five steps proposed in the chapter are the most difficult ones to understand? Which do you anticipate will be the one most difficult to undertake?
3. Which of the five steps are you already in the habit of doing?
4. Can you explain how this method differs from the way theologians do theology?

# Notes

## Chapter 1 / Meaning and Work

1. Studs Terkel, *Working* (New York: Pantheon Books, 1972). passim.
2. Michael Maccoby, *Why Work: Leading the New Generation* (New York, Simon and Schuster, 1988).
3. Ibid, pp. 54–59.
4. Ibid, p. 80.
5. Ibid, p. 119.
6. Ibid, p. 133.
7. Ibid, p. 137.
8. Ibid, p. 152.
9. Ibid, p. 156.
10. Ibid, p. 88.
11. Ibid, p. 115.
12. Ibid, p. 177.
13. Ibid, p. 29.
14. Ibid, p. 42.
15. E. F. Schumacher and Peter Gillingham, *Good Work* (San Francisco: Harper and Row, 1980), p. 7.
16. Adam Smith, *Wealth of Nations* (New York: Penguin Books, 1982), p. 81.
17. Schumacher, *Good Work*, pp. 45–46.
18. Ibid., p. 47.
19. Dorothee Soelle, *To Work and to Love* (Philadelphia: Fortress Press, 1984), p. 84.
20. Peter Maurin, *Easy Essays* (Chicago: Franciscan Herald Press, 1961), p. 53.
21. Ibid., p. 54.

## Chapter 2 / The Creator God and Working People

1. Bertell Ollman, *Alienation: Marx's Conception of Man in Capitalist Society* (Cambridge: Cambridge University Press, 1975), p. 133.

163

2. Ibid., p. 134.

3. Ibid.

4. W. J. Heisler, "Worker Alienation: 1900–1975," and Stanislav B. Kosl, "Work and Mental Health: Contemporary Research Evidence," in *A Matter of Dignity*, ed. Heisler and Houck.

5. Erich Fromm, *The Sane Society* (New York: Reinhart and Winston, 1955), p. 28.

6. Paul Ricoeur, *The Symbolism of Evil* (Boston: Beacon Press, 1978), p. 15.

7. Bernard Lonergan, S.J., *Insight: A Study of Human Understanding* (New York: Philosophical Library, 1958), pp. 596–98.

8. Dorothee Soelle, *To Work and to Love* (Philadelphia: Fortress Press, 1984), pp. 17–18.

9. John C. Haughey, S.J., *The Holy Use of Money* (Garden City, NY: Doubleday, 1986; repr. Crossroad, 1989), chapter 1.

10. National Conference of Catholic Bishops, *Economic Justice for All: Pastoral Letter on Catholic Social Teaching and the U.S. Economy* (Washington, D.C.: National Conference of Catholic Bishops, 1986), no. 80.

11. There are many authors taking this tack, for example, Joyce Little, "Sexual Equality in the Church: A Theological Resolution to an Anthropological Dilemma," *The Heythrop Journal* 28 (April 1987): 165–78.

12. *Economic Justice for All*, no. 301.

13. Stakeholders are all who have a stake in a corporation's decisions; these would be the consumers, the employees, the suppliers, the immediate community.

14. Patricia Werhane, *Persons, Rights and Corporations* (Englewood Cliffs, NJ: Prentice-Hall, 1985), passim; M. Gibson, *Workers' Rights* Totowa, NJ: Rowman and Allanheld, 1983), passim.

15. John Paul II, *On Human Work*, no. 6, in *Origins* 11, no. 15 (September 24, 1981).

16. Ibid., no. 7.

17. Soelle, *To Work and to Love*, p. 38.

18. Ernest Becker, *The Denial of Death* (New York: Free Press 1973), chapter 1.

19. Gerhard Von Rad, *Genesis* (Philadelphia: Westminister Press, 1963), passim.

## Chapter 3 / Work and Rest

1. Henricus Renckens, S.J., *Israel's Concept of the Beginning* (New York: Herder and Herder, 1964), p. 103.

2. Abraham Joshua Heschel, *The Sabbath* (New York: Farrar, Straus & Giroux, 1975), p. 43.

3. Ibid., p. 52.

4. Josef Pieper, *Leisure: The Basis of Culture* (New York: New American Library, 1964), p. 33.

5. Ascending Christology is an effort to appreciate the humanity of Jesus and his human consciousness. Giants in this recovery are Karl Rahner and Bernard Lonergan who dispelled a crudely mythological interpretation of the Incarnation and updated the meaning of person used by the Council of Chalcedon. And, of course, the scriptural renewal assisted mightily in this as in all other aspects of the renewal of theology and church life.

6. Heschel, *Sabbath*, p. 61.

7. Renckens, *Beginning*, p. 101.

8. *The New American Bible* (New York: Catholic Book Publishing Co., 1970), footnote on Mark 2:28.

9. Son of Man is used eighty-six times in the New Testament. It is used to describe his earthly work, his suffering, and his eschatological function. Its use by Jesus and of Jesus synthesized Old Testament and Apocryphal uses. See David M. Stanley, S. J., and Raymond E. Brown, S. S., "Aspects of New Testament Thought," nos. 28–30, in *The Jerome Biblical Commentary*, ed. Raymond E. Brown, Joseph A. Fitzmyer, and Roland E. Murphy (Englewood Cliffs, NJ: Prentice-Hall, 1968), vol. 2, p. 773.

10. Especially Daniel 7:13–14.

11. The Greek *kopiontes* is rendered *labor* by most English translators of the New Testament. *The New American Bible* translates it *weary*.

12. Winton V. Solberg, *Redeem the Time: The Puritan Sabbath in Early America* (Cambridge: Harvard University Press 1977), p. 12.

13. Ibid., p. 14.

## Chapter 4 / The God Who Works

1. Louis J. Puhl, S.J. *Spiritual Exercises of St. Ignatius* (Chicago: Loyola University Press, 1951), no. 236.

2. Ibid., no. 233.

3. Ibid., no. 236.

4. William J. Young, *St. Ignatius' Own Story* (Chicago: Loyola University Press, 1980), p. 103 (letter of Ignatius to Father Brandao).

5. Ibid., p. 103.

6. Ibid., p. 104.

7. Ignatius of Loyola, *The Constitutions of the Society of Jesus*, trans.

George E. Ganss, S. J. (St. Louis: Institute of Jesuit Sources, 1970), no. 282 of the Constitutions, Part III.

8. Young, *St. Ignatius' Own Story*, pp. 69–70.

9. Loyola, *Constitutions*, no. 250.

10. Loyola, *Constitutions*, no. 288.

11. Michael J. Buckley, S. J., "Ecumenism and Jesuit Spirituality," in *Centro Ignatiana Spirituali*, February 1989, p. 5.

12. Puhl, *Spiritual Exercises*, no. 237.

13. Gerhard Von Rad, *Wisdom in Creation* (London: SCM Press, 1972), p. 165.

14. See, for example, John R. Sachs, "Glory," in *The New Dictionary of Theology*, p. 417–20.

15. *Decree on the Apostolate of the Laity*, no. 7, in *Documents of Vatican II*, ed. Abbott, p. 497.

16. Lonergan, *Insight*, p. 597.

17. Puhl, *Spiritual Exercises*, no. 95.

18. Ibid., no. 96.

## Chapter 5 / Evil at Work

1. John Paul II, *On Human Work*, no. 12, in *Origins* 11, no. 15 (September 24, 1981).

2. Ibid., no. 14.

3. Josef Tischner, *The Spirit of Solidarity* (New York: Harper and Row, 1984), p. 13.

4. John Paul II, *On Human Work*, no. 13.

5. Edgar H. Schein, *Organizational Culture and Leadership* (San Francisco: Jossey-Bass Publishers, 1986), p. 9.

6. John Paul II, *On Human Work*, no. 13.

7. Ibid.

8. Charles K. Wilbur, "Economic Theory and the Common Good," in *The Common Good and U. S. Capitalism*, ed. Oliver Williams and John Houck (Lanham, MD: University Press of America, 1987), pp. 245–46.

9. Ralph McInerny, "The Primacy of the Common Good," in *The Common Good*, p. 73.

10. Walter Wink, *Unmasking the Powers* (Philadelphia: Fortress Press, 1986), p. 4.

11. Ibid., p. 69.

12. Ibid., p. 93.

13. Ibid., p. 93.

14. Ibid., p. 92.

15. Ibid., p. 79.

16. Ibid., p. 107.
17. Ibid., p. 107.
18. Ibid., p. 73.
19. Puhl, *Spiritual Exercises*, no. 146.
20. Ibid.
21. Novak has elaborated on this theme in his *Spirit of Democratic Capitalism* (New York: Simon and Schuster, 1982) and *Freedom with Justice* (San Francisco: Harper and Row, 1984).
22. Quoted from Michael Hines and Kenneth Himes, "The Myth of Self-Interest," *Commonweal*, September 23, 1988, p. 494.
23. Ibid., p. 495.
24. Quoted from Michael Novak, "Structures of Virtue, Structures of Sin," *America*, January 28, 1989, p. 57.
25. Anne Wilson Schaef and Diane Fassel, *The Addictive Organization* (San Francisco: Harper and Row, 1988), p. 4.
26. Ibid., p. 68.
27. Ibid., chapter 3.
28. Ibid., p. 65.
29. Ibid., p. 65–66.
30. Ibid., pp. 129–36.
31. John Paul II, *On Social Concerns*, no. 38, in *Origins* 17, no. 40 (March 3, 1988).
32. Ibid., no. 35.
33. Ibid., no. 38.
34. Ibid.
35. Ibid.
36. Ibid.

## Chapter 6 / What Work Lasts?

1. McBrien, *Catholicism*, pp. 1101 ff.
2. John J. Collins, "Apocalyptic," in *The New Dictionary of Theology*, pp. 42–43.
3. Miroslav Wolf, "Work in the Spirit," unpublished manuscript.
4. *Decree on the Apostolate of the Laity*, no. 5, in *Documents of Vatican II*, ed. Abbott, p. 495.
5. *Pastoral Constitution on the Church in the Modern World*, no. 39, *Documents*, p. 237.
6. Ibid.
7. Jürgen Moltmann, *Theology of Hope* (New York: Harper and Row, 1967), p. 33.

8. Johannes B. Metz, *Theology of the World* (New York: Herder and Herder, 1969), p. 82.

9. Ibid., p. 89.

10. Ibid., p. 144.

11. Teilhard de Chardin, *The Divine Milieu* (New York: Harper and Row, 1960), p. 29.

12. Evolution was for Teilhard a "combination of the play of chance (which is physical) and that of finality (which is psychic)" (Teilhard, *Human Energy* [New York: Harcourt, Brace and Jovanovich, 1969], p. 72).

13. Teilhard de Chardin, *Hymn of the Universe* (New York: Harper and Row, 1965), p. 19–37.

14. Teilhard, *The Divine Milieu*, p. 144.

15. Ibid.

16. Ibid., p. 15.

17. Harvey Egan, S. J., *Christian Mysticism* (New York: Pueblo Publishing Co., 1984), p. 285.

18. Christopher Mooney, S. J., *Teilhard de Chardin and the Mystery of Christ* (Garden City, NY: Doubleday, 1968), pp. 189–90.

19. Teilhard, *The Divine Milieu*, p. 64.

20. Mooney, *Teilhard de Chardin*, p. 153.

21. Teilhard, *The Divine Milieu*, p. 55.

22. Ibid., p. 55.

23. Ibid., p. 56.

24. Egan, *Christian Mysticism*, pp. 266–67.

25. Teilhard de Chardin, *Writings in Time of War* (New York: Harper and Row, 1968), pp. 39–40.

26. "Our actions actually form the cosmic Christ" (Egan, *Christian Mysticism*, p. 272).

27. Mooney, *Teilhard de Chardin*, p. 190.

28. Egan, *Christian Mysticism*, p. 286.

29. Teilhard, *Writings in Time of War*, p. 39.

30. Teilhard, *The Divine Milieu*, p. 125.

31. Teilhard, *Hymn of the Universe*, p. 14.

32. "Mass on the World" is an essay in *Hymn of the Universe*, p. 22.

33. Ibid., p. 23.

## Chapter 7 / The Meaning God Sees

1. Franz Jozef van Beeck, S. J., *Christ Proclaimed* (Ramsey, NJ: Paulist Press, 1979).

2. *Dogmatic Constitution on the Church*, no. 34, *Documents of Vatican II*, ed. Abbott, p. 60.

3. Birger Gerhardsson, *The Ethos of the Bible* (Philadelphia: Fortress Press, 1981), p. 30.

4. James L. Muyskens, *The Sufficiency of Hope* (Philadelphia: Temple University Press, 1979), pp. 16–17.

## Chapter 8 / A Spirituality of Work

1. A good definition of contributive justice may be found in *Economic Justice for All: Pastoral Letter on Catholic Social Teaching and the U.S. Economy* (Washington, DC: National Conference of Catholic Bishops, 1986): *"[P]ersons have an obligation to be active and productive participants in the life of society and that society has a duty to enable them to participate in this way"* (no. 71).

2. Hannah Arendt, *The Human Condition* (New York: Doubleday, 1959), p. 74.

3. Richard McBrien, *Catholicism* (San Francisco: Harper and Row, 1981), pp. 1141–42.

4. Francis Schüssler Fiorenza, "Work and Critical Theology," in *A Matter of Dignity*, ed. W. J. Heisler and John W. Houck (Notre Dame, IN: University of Notre Dame Press, 1977), p. 37.

5. Robert N. Bellah, "Resurrecting the Common Good," *Commonweal*, December 18, 1987, p. 736.

6. W.H.C. Frend, *Martyrdom and Persecution in the Early Church* (New York: Anchor Books, 1967), pp. 82–83.

7. Joann Wolski Conn, "Spirituality," in *The New Dictionary of Theology*, ed. Joseph A. Komonchak, Mary Collins, and Dermot A. Lane (Wilmington, DE: Michael Glazier, 1987), pp. 974–75.

8. Paul Ricoeur, *The Conflict of Interpretations: Essays in Hermeneutics* (Evanston, IL: Northwestern University Press, 1976), p. 87.

## Chapter 9 / A Method

1. Clodovis Boff, *Theology and Praxis* (Maryknoll, NY: Orbis Books, 1987), chapter 1.

2. Louis J. Puhl, S.J., *The Spiritual Exercises of St. Ignatius* (Chicago: Loyola University Press, 1951), section 313.

3. Joseph Cardijn, *Challenge to Action* (Chicago: Fides Publishers, 1955), p. 86.

4. Ibid., p. 87.

5. Philip Berryman, *Liberation Theology* (New York: Pantheon Books, 1987).

6. Ibid., pp. 35–37.

7. Thomas H. Groome, *Christian Religious Education* (San Francisco: Harper and Row, 1980), especially chapter 10.

8. Edward Farley, "Interpreting Situations: An Inquiry into the Notion of Practical Theology," in *Formation and Reflection*, ed. Lewis Mudge and James Poling (Philadelphia: Fortress Press, 1987), p. 9.

9. Ibid., p. 9.

10. Ibid., p. 10.

11. Ibid., p. 11.

12. Ibid., p. 10.

# Index

171